Praise for *The Greatest Ponzi Scheme on Earth*

"Packed with evidence about the benefits of spending restraint and pro-growth tax policy."

—LARRY KUDLOW, Former Director of the National Economic Council under President Donald Trump

"Great real-world examples of how nations can prosper...but also tragic examples of how tax-and-spend policies lead to economic decline."

—ART LAFFER, Former member of President Ronald Reagan's Economic Policy Advisory Board, Creator of the Laffer Curve

"Wake up, America! As Rubin and Mitchell demonstrate, bad fiscal policy is stymying economic growth and putting us perilously close to economic calamity. Fortunately, they show how we can get out of this mess!"

—JIM MILLER, Former Director of the Office of Management and Budget under President Ronald Reagan

"The authors not only lucidly lay out the increasingly critical state of Washington's finances, but they also offer up exciting, pro-growth, politically appealing policies to crush this crisis. We ignore this ever-so-timely book at our peril."

—STEVE FORBES, Editor-in-Chief of *Forbes* magazine

"*The Greatest Ponzi Scheme on Earth* is the best single book on the coming fiscal disaster yet written. The authors are driven by data rather than emotion. They detail how the US and most other major countries have ended up on an unsustainable spending binge. But they also give us a ray of hope by presenting corrective actions that may be politically doable before we go over the cliff."

—RICHARD RAHN, Former Chief Economist of the U.S. Chamber of Commerce

"Everyone knows that the mountain of debt spending in Washington will collapse as any Ponzi scheme always does. When it does, the collapse will cause financial havoc, and everyone will get flattened. When Bernie Madoff ran his scheme, we put him in jail and threw away the key. After reading this book you will think that is what we should do with the spendaholics in Congress."

—**STEPHEN MOORE,** Heritage Foundation economist

"Both parties are spending like there's no tomorrow. Debts and deficits have continued to grow out of control no matter who is in charge. There's still time, but if the fiscal problems aren't fixed soon, we'll face a fiscal bomb that will destroy the economy and our country for future generations. Rubin and Mitchell explain the problems and solutions in a way that anyone can understand. Every voter should read this book and then send to their representatives to fix this mess now."

—**CHRIS BALL,** Ph.D., Istvan Szechenyi Chair in International Economics and Director of the Central European Institute, Quinnipiac University

The Greatest
Ponzi
Scheme
on Earth

How the US Can Avoid
Economic Collapse

Leslie A. Rubin and **Daniel J. Mitchell**

FOREWORD BY Hon. David M. Walker, Former US Comptroller General

Published by Worth Books, an imprint of Forefront Books.
Distributed by Simon & Schuster.

Library of Congress Control Number: 2023923589

Print ISBN: 978-1-63763-277-2
E-book ISBN: 978-1-63763-278-9

Cover Design by Faceout Studio, Amanda Hudson
Interior Design by Bill Kersey, KerseyGraphics

Printed in the United States of America

Pon·zi scheme

noun

A form of fraud in which belief in the success of a non-existent enterprise is fostered by the payment of quick returns to the first investors from money invested by later investors.

Is the United States' debt a Ponzi scheme? The federal debt is sold to investors with the promise to pay them back in the future. But, practically speaking, there is no source of income from which to do that. It can only be paid back by borrowing more money from future investors.

Does that make it a Ponzi scheme? You be the judge.

The most significant threat to our national security is our debt.

—ADMIRAL MIKE MULLEN,

CHAIRMAN OF THE JOINT CHIEFS OF STAFF, 2010

Contents

Section IV: Common Sense Solutions

Authors' Note

Before we get started, let us tell you a short story. It is a real-life drama about what can happen when an economy goes down a path of ill-conceived economic policy and short-term thinking. It is not pretty, and it is really happening in many countries, all in various stages of decline.

Greece

Greece is a modern European country with roots going back to early civilization.

Imagine being a resident of Greece in 2007. Life seems good. Your nation's economy has been enjoying strong growth, with annual inflation-adjusted GDP rising by an average of more than 4 percent over the previous ten years. You have a job, the sunshine is warm, and the government provides you with lots of goodies.

But there are some annoying people who don't want to enjoy life. These Cassandras endlessly complain about government being too big. They whine that the government is spending too much, and that it is irresponsible to finance a big chunk of that spending with debt. They also make wonky arguments about an aging population and excessive levels of dependency.

You dismiss their warnings. After all, some professor during your college years said that government spending is good for the economy. That professor also said that government debt is irrelevant because "it's just money we owe ourselves." You pay attention to financial markets, and you can see that investors trust your government. How do you know this? Because they are buying Greek bonds that barely pay more interest than ultrasafe German bonds.

So you can comfortably ignore the Cassandras and their boring arguments about fiscal and demographic trends. Or so you think.

The following year saw the beginnings of what would become a global financial crisis. At first, it didn't seem too bad. The economy shrank in 2008, but by less than 1 percent. But the situation worsened in 2009.

Skittish investors began to worry that the Greek government was facing multiple problems—too much spending, too much debt, a weak national economy, and a weak global economy. What if the combination of those factors meant that the government could not be trusted to make promised payments on government bonds? Was there a risk of an Argentine-style default, even though everything had looked rosy just two years earlier?

The answer was yes to both questions. Investors started to dump their Greek government bonds. Interest rates spiked because of the perceived risk. Greece had fulfilled Margaret Thatcher's warning—they ran out of other people's money.

In 2007, most people in Greece probably thought that they would be immune from fiscal and economic calamity. They were wrong, and they paid a heavy price. What's tragic is that the horrible consequences could have been avoided with a modest level of spending restraint over the preceding few years.

The rest of the story is very grim. Greece had to get multiple bailouts over the next few years. Its economy suffered a deep depression, and living standards have still not recovered.

Why are we explaining Greece? Why are we being the "annoying people"? Because we want to be the Cassandras, but hopefully with more success. We want to avert a fiscal disaster before it is too late.

The fact is, this awful series of events could happen in the United States. Maybe not next year. Maybe not even next decade. But sooner or later, bad trends and perceived risk become awful reality. The question for the United States is whether our politicians will make the responsible choice that Greek politicians failed to make.

Why Are We Writing This Book?

Most informed US citizens understand that there are problems with the debt and deficit. But few are aware of the magnitude and severity of the problem and what the future will be if we "keep on keeping on." In response, we are writing this simple, short book to alert, alarm, and move to action the concerned citizens of this country who care about our future.

There have been plenty of past warnings. How many times have we heard that the sky is falling? A book was written about the imminent collapse in 1995.[1] In 2010, the chairman of the Joint Chiefs of Staff stated, "The biggest danger to our national security is our national debt." Well-regarded senator Tom Coburn cowrote *The Debt Bomb* in 2012. Perhaps most damning, the Department of the Treasury unequivocally states in its published financial statements: "The current fiscal policy is unsustainable."

A key measure of the problem is the amount of interest-bearing debt and the ratio of that to the total economy, the GDP (Gross Domestic Product).

	Debt	Ratio
In 1960 it was	286 Billion	54%
In 1974 it was	475 Billion	31% (low point)
In 1995 it was	5.0 Trillion	64%
In 2008 it was	10.0 Trillion	68%
In 2010 it was	13.6 Trillion	90%
In 2012 it was	16.1 Trillion	99%
In 2020 it was	27.7 Trillion	129% (high point)
In 2022 it was	30.8 Trillion	123%

But these numbers merely show existing debt. The Department of the Treasury reports that, as of September 30, 2022, the total debt of the US, including unfunded obligations[2] of Social Security and Medicare, was $122 trillion: 490 percent of GDP.

---

1 Harry Figgie, *Bankruptcy 1995: The Coming Collapse of America and How to Stop It* (New York: Little Brown and Company, 1992).
2 Unfunded obligations are the shortfall of future revenue against planned payments.

The Congressional Budget Office (CBO) projects federal deficits averaging $2 trillion per year (and interest-bearing debt over $50 trillion) in ten years under current policy and programs—assuming no new programs are implemented. The interest on this debt will come to another $2 trillion per year.

Get the picture yet?

Overview

This book is written for you, the voting public, the folks on Main Street. Our objective is to educate (not indoctrinate) about economic policies that will move this country toward prosperity and growth without taking us over the fiscal cliff.

In section I, "The United States Is Bankrupt," we explain the financial condition of this country and what is driving our fiscal problems.

In section II, "Real-World Fiscal Lessons," we illustrate and explain economic successes and failures and the policies that led to those good or bad results. We also analyze some key periods in US economic history to explain what went wrong or right, and why.

In section III, "What the Hell Can We Do about It?," we suggest some of the key areas that need to be fixed and conceptual ideas as to how to do it.

In section IV, "Common Sense Solutions," we summarize the key, proven elements of how to grow an economy and improve the standard of living for everyone. We then suggest an approach to moving forward to get the job done.

These lessons matter, and they matter increasingly as the debt grows and the population ages. This is dark stuff, but we hope you will find it interesting and thought-provoking. Most of all, we hope you enjoy it and learn from it, then take action at the voting booth.

Leslie A. Rubin, Founder,
Main Street Economics, Inc.
*Main Street Economics is a public service,
nonpartisan, nonprofit organization.*

Daniel J. Mitchell, President,
Center for Freedom and Prosperity, Inc.
*Center for Freedom and Prosperity
is a nonprofit organization.*

Foreword

The *Greatest Ponzi Scheme on Earth* is intended to be a wake-up call and a call-to-action regarding our nation's expanding government, huge deficits, and mounting debt burdens. The authors are Les Rubin, a successful entrepreneur who has a talent for writing in clear and plain English, and Dan Mitchell, a respected economist with significant experience in connection with federal fiscal issues.

I agreed to write this foreword because the book's authors and I share at least three things in common. First, we love our country. Second, we believe that significant fiscal reforms are needed to stem America's decline and create a better future. Third, we believe that citizen education and engagement is an essential element to achieve the needed reforms.

The sad but simple truth is that America is in decline—but we can turn it around. We are currently flying blind in mountains of debt without a plan to achieve a soft landing. As you will find out in this book, the federal government has grown too big, promised too much, subsidized too many, and has lost control of the budget. Debt burdens are already too high and are rising rapidly. Shockingly, interest is the federal government's fastest growing expense. And what do we get for interest? Nothing!

Neither major political party has been fiscally responsible in the past two decades, and we have too many career politicians who are focused on their next election rather than the next generation. Stated differently: too many people are living for today rather than trying to take steps to create a better tomorrow for our country, children, grandchildren, and future generations of Americans. Our current fiscal path is irresponsible, unethical, and immoral, and *we must change course.*

The Greatest Ponzi Scheme on Earth provides a range of facts to demonstrate that we are on an unsustainable fiscal path, which has been acknowledged by every major federal fiscal and monetary agency. While our primary problem is escalating federal spending, some additional revenues will be needed to achieve bipartisan support. Therefore, we must make tough budget control, spending reduction, and revenue enhancement choices to save our future, and we should do so sooner versus later.

These steps coupled with regulatory relief, education reform, immigration reform, and other actions are needed to increase economic growth and individual opportunity, and to maintain our status as the world's leading superpower.

This book also provides several illustrative solutions that should be considered and some ideas on how best to achieve them. It recognizes that the people are ahead of the politicians.

Americans know that tough choices are needed and are willing to accept them if they are part of a comprehensive, goal-based plan that is consistent with principles and values that bring people together rather than divide them apart. My 2012 national fiscal responsibility bus tour, titled the $10 Million a Minute Tour, proved this to be true. Unfortunately, we are in much worse shape now than then.

When thinking about our future, we must learn from the past and others. For example, Rome was a great superpower in the past, but Rome fell for several reasons: fiscal irresponsibility, political incivility, moral decline, overextended military, and the inability to control its borders. Do these sound familiar?

In his farewell address, President George Washington issued four warnings. He advised us to avoid excessive debt, foreign wars, regionalism, and factionalism (e.g., political parties). How are we doing?

On a more positive note, Switzerland was on a declining fiscal path in the 1990s. However, in 2001, 84.7 percent of its citizens voted to adopt a constitutional amendment that limited growth in federal spending and constrained debt levels to reasonable and sustainable levels of the economy. As a result, Switzerland now has among the highest incomes per capita, a strong and stable currency, and the highest debt rating of any major sovereign nation. It is financially strong today and has a sound and sustainable fiscal path for the future. The US needs to adopt an appropriate fiscal responsibility constitutional amendment as well.

We must learn from history and learn from others. After all, no country is exempt from the laws of prudent finance, including the United States.

In the final analysis, if we want to create a better future, the first three words of preamble to the Constitution must come alive: "We the People." We the people are responsible for who we elect to represent us, and we will suffer the consequences if they fail to act to address this large, known, and growing financial challenge.

Concerned Americans need to become informed regarding the challenges we face and options to address them. *The Greatest Ponzi Scheme on Earth* will help in that regard. Americans need to pressure their elected representatives to act in a timely and responsible manner. And if they fail to do so, the people need to elect representatives who will. This is a key element to returning to a republic that is truly representative of and responsive to the general public rather than the "wingnuts" in both major parties and the special interests who are concerned about their narrow interests rather than broader public interest.

The three of us are committed to do our part. All that we ask is that you do yours. If you want to do more, check out www.MainStreetEconomics.org.

Hon. David M. Walker
Former Comptroller General of the United States
Alexandria, Virginia

Introduction

America, we have a problem. It is serious, you need to understand it, and we all need to fix it. The US Ship of State is sailing into troubled waters, headed directly for the proverbial iceberg. If you do not understand this reality, then you need to read this book. It will alert and alarm you, and then you will understand why we need to course correct if we are to survive as a nation. We are all guilty of complacency, but the numbers and projections should shake us out of our torpor.

First, we need to understand the problem, then understand that there are logical fixes. Then we must demand that our representatives apply those fixes before it is too late.

But when will the you-know-what hit the fan? When it does, will the United States suffer some sort of fiscal collapse? In short, is America in trouble? We think so. And we think something bad will happen if policy does not change. We don't know when the crisis will occur. It may be in ten years, it may be in thirty—but it's coming.

Here are two calculations, easy to understand and extremely disconcerting:

1. Since America's last budget surplus in 2000, federal government spending has increased by an average of 6.1 percent per year while the economy (our GDP) has grown by only 4.3 percent per year.

2. According to Congressional Budget Office projections, federal spending over the next thirty years will grow by an average of more than 4.4 percent per year while the economy will grow by less than 3.8 percent per year.

Simply stated, America got in trouble because government grew too fast. And we are headed for more trouble in the future because government is projected to continue growing too fast. Indeed, the most important message in this book is this: good fiscal policy is when government spending grows slower than the private sector. That's it. Conversely, bad fiscal policy is when government spending grows faster than the private sector. Simple as that.

When there is bad fiscal policy (government growing too fast), bad things happen: taxes go up, deficits increase, and there is greater risk of inflationary monetary policy. All of those can be avoided if politicians show some spending discipline.

Here's another number that merits attention. The federal government has tens of trillions of dollars in unfunded obligations. That wonky term refers to all future spending that's been promised for programs such as Medicare and Social Security, above and beyond future tax revenues. Those obligations are not the same as legally binding debt. After all, Congress can simply change laws to make the unfunded liabilities disappear. But political pressure always pushes in the other direction.

Let's look at the issue from that perspective. Pretend the federal government is a household. If your family spends more than it earns, it has a shortfall that it puts on the family credit card. This is now a debt the family owes. If the family continues to do that, the debt grows. At some point the family can no longer afford to pay the credit card company, and the creditor stops issuing new debt. The family is bankrupt. It is a story as old as time. Everyone gets it—except the politicians in Washington.

There are a few "green eyeshade" types who look closely at America's budget numbers. What do they say? "The current fiscal path is unsustainable." This is a quote from the *Executive Summary of the United States Financial Statements* prepared by the Department of the Treasury.[3]

To fully understand the comment, let's make it more relatable. Let's take the information from the US financial statements for September 30, 2022, and scale it down to your household. To do that we will delete eight zeros from the actual data and pretend it is your family's financial situation. And pay attention—these number crunches include unfunded obligations.

---

3   *Executive Summary to the Fiscal Year 2022 Financial Report of U.S. Government*, prepared by the US Department of the Treasury, (Washington, DC, 2022), https://www.fiscal.treasury.gov/reports-statements/financial-report/unsustainable-fiscal-path.html.

REVENUE/CREDIT CARD DATA	US Financial Info	Your Household
Revenue (Fiscal 9/30/22)	$4,925,900,000,000	$49,259
Expenses (Fiscal 9/30/22)	$6,301,400,000,000	$63,014
Net Loss	($1,375,500,000,000)	($13,755)
Credit Card Balance (9/30/21)	$28,500,000,000,000	$285,000
Addition to Credit Card in 2022	$2,500,000,000,000	$25,000
New Credit Card Balance (9/30/22)	$31,000,000,000,000	$310,000

BALANCE SHEET DATA		
Assets (9/30/22)	$4,962,400,000,000	$49,624
Liabilities (Per 9/30/22 Statement)	$39,022,300,000,000	$390,223
Unrecorded Debt to Trust Funds	$6,700,000,000,000	$67,000
Unfunded Obligations (SS/Medicare)	$75,900,000,000,000	$759,000
Total Liabilities	$121,622,300,000,000	$1,216,223
Net Worth	($116,659,900,000,000)	($1,166,599)

"Revenue/Credit Card Data" only includes interest-bearing debt for the US. Excluded are the regular liabilities incurred in the ordinary course of business ($14.7 trillion) and unfunded obligations (future promises to spend money currently exceed future revenue collection by $75.9 trillion).

A key metric of the health of an economy is the interest-bearing debt to GDP ratio. It has historically ranged from 30–65 percent (from 1960 to 2008), which is a manageable ratio. But since 2008, the interest-bearing debt to GDP ratio has ballooned to almost 130 percent.

Gaining Control

We must get control of the fiscal affairs of this country, but that is easier said than done. The best answers come from the real world: what has worked well and what hasn't. What you will see in section II of this book is that countries with limited government grow faster and have a higher standard of living. The formula for growth is clear, and we will explain why.

The right approach to a more prosperous America is to control government spending, but that doesn't mean we shouldn't have welfare and support programs. We became a wealthy country with limited government, but we have gone off the rails with expensive programs that do not properly meet their own goals. We need to reform or eliminate some programs so we can be fiscally responsible and move to reduce the cost of government to match our income. That will lead to faster growth and more prosperity for all. It can be done, and we cover the most important programs to address in section III to explain how.

Got it? The message is still very simple. You are bankrupt, and so is the US. But the United States is still living on credit because it has an AA credit rating and can still borrow or print money. The US credit card company is still funding. Yours is not. You are bankrupt, the US keeps on borrowing, and it will until . . . it cannot.

Who's Funding This?

The federal government borrows funds to pay for the deficits from you and me and private investors. We are the bank, and the government is borrowing money from us. Any decent banker will eventually ask what should have been their first question: "How are you going to pay me back?"

Nowadays, the federal government never has a surplus (net income); it has only deficits (losses) and will for the foreseeable future. It cannot repay the debt—as would be required by any bank. The only answer the government can offer is to borrow more to pay you back. That, my fellow citizens, is called a Ponzi scheme. There is no source of income for the US to repay the debt other than to borrow more money.

This book is simply a story about the United States. Where we have been. Where we are. Where we are headed. And what happens if our credit card gets maxed out and the greatest Ponzi scheme on Earth comes to an end. It is no longer a question of *if* the credit card maxes out, but *when* that day will come if we remain on our current course.

Are we going to let our Ship of State crash into the proverbial iceberg? It is up to us to determine that. The problem is fixable, but only if we have the will to make difficult choices. My generation inherited a country that worked, and we owe it to the younger generations, our kids and grandkids, to leave them one that still works.

Who We Are

The authors of this book have very different backgrounds.

Daniel J. Mitchell is a professional economist. He holds a PhD from George Mason University and has been working on fiscal policy for four decades. He's worked for taxpayer groups, for think tanks, and for the United States Senate. He has spoken on fiscal issues in the United States and more than sixty other nations, and he's written for all the major newspapers and appeared on all the major TV networks.

Leslie A. Rubin is a businessman and entrepreneur. His education is in accounting, with a business degree from the University of North Carolina at Chapel Hill. He worked as a professional accountant/controller for a decade and as a real estate developer for years; he understands a balance sheet, an income statement, and financial projections, and has overseen the repayment of borrowed money for over half a century.

Both of us see the same picture, and that is why we are alarmed. This book is meant to alert and alarm you as well. Pay attention, and you will agree with our thoughts and concerns. Then heed our call and let your representatives in DC know your opinion. They will not address this problem without public pressure.

Take the time to read this short book; it is written for you, the voting public of the United States. Become a part of the Main Street lobby. Go to our website, www.mainstreeteconomics.org, and Contact Congress. Just enter your name and address and hit Send. You can use our message or write your own. Call them. Express your opinions. Together we can move this country forward toward fiscal sanity, growth, and a higher standard of living for all.

Learn economics, then vote smart.

SECTION I

The United States Is Bankrupt

Overview

This section explains America's current fiscal situation. The key point to under-stand is that we have deep financial problems that are masked because our national credit card still works. The US is the strongest, largest economy in the world, and our money is the international standard. As such, our debt is considered very safe, and there are plenty of domestic and foreign buyers whenever the US Treasury issues more debt.

But are we really that strong? Is any country that strong? We have a big economy, but people in Greece thought their economy was doing fine twenty years ago, only to see everything spin out of control very quickly. While the United States is surely in better shape than Greece, you will learn in this section that America's debt and financial future are still very troubling. It is plain to see that we must correct course, or there will be serious economic consequences in the future. The longer we wait to address these issues, the harder and more economically painful it will be to fix them.

So what has driven us to this condition, and where we are headed? That is the subject of this first section.

Chapter 1: "The Current US Situation." In this chapter we will present exactly where we are as of the financial year that ended on September 30, 2022: the last audited financial statements prepared by the Department of the Treasury as of this writing.[4]

Chapter 2: "America's Spending Crisis." The limited government envi-sioned by our Founding Fathers is a distant memory. Our spending is out of control, and we continue to add programs that we have no means to pay for other than borrowing more money.

4 Audited by the GAO: Government Accountability Office.

Chapter 3: "Deficits and Projections." This is an overview of the current year's deficit—the makeup of the revenue and expenses—to show how we got here. The good news is that the deficit for fiscal 2022 has been reduced by over $1 trillion as a result of the extraordinary COVID-related expenses expiring. But it is still a $1.5 trillion deficit, and the really bad news is that it is rising rapidly in 2023. The latest projections from the CBO show the deficit continuing to grow indefinitely. This leads to more debt, more interest expense, a bigger deficit, and ... more debt. This is a vicious cycle, known as the doom loop, that we must break, or the Ponzi scheme will eventually fail.

Chapter 4: "Key Drivers of the Deficits." This chapter focuses on the spending issues that are the main drivers of the deficits. First and foremost are the so-called "entitlements." The word is probably a misnomer—we are not entitled to anything that we have not paid for.

Chapter 5: "Entitlements." This chapter details the specifics of enti-tlements, as they comprise the major part of the expenditures and are the biggest driver of the deficit.

Chapter 6: "What Happens If ..." The Ponzi scheme fails when the inves-tors who buy our debt are no longer willing to do so. If we are ever unable to borrow money to fund our deficits, there are two choices, neither of them desirable. 1) The Federal Reserve can simply print money to cover the deficits. This is not a long-range solution and will lead to extraordinary inflation. 2) We can honor our debts as required by law and simply cut everything else until we have a forced, balanced budget. That would lead to economic depression. The only other possibility is to default on the debt—simply do not pay it as scheduled. That would also lead to severe worldwide consequences.

We must understand the situation in objective terms if we are to fix these problems. If you are a concerned citizen, please keep reading. We will need an educated citizenry if we are to tackle the tough choices that lie ahead.

CHAPTER 1

The Current US Situation

America's debt spiked dramatically during WWII to more than 100 percent of gross domestic product (GDP), which is the size of a nation's economy. After the war, though, America's debt burden dropped—but not because we actually reduced the debt. Yes, there were a few years with budget surpluses, especially in the late 1940s, but there were also a few years with budget deficits. In 1962, the debt was slightly higher than it was in 1946.

So why did the debt burden fall? Because our economy grew faster than the red ink. Between 1947 and 1962, federal debt grew by about 11 percent, but the economy grew by more than 150 percent. As a result, the debt to GDP ratio dropped significantly, as the following chart indicates:

Government Debt Climbs to WWII Levels

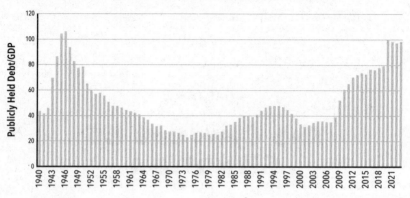

While there are no magical answers as to what amount of debt is correct, generally we want to measure it as a ratio of debt to GDP and keep it at a reasonable level: ideally less than 50 percent of economic output. Debt may continue to grow, but if it grows at a slower rate than the economy, it will decline as a percentage of GDP. If deficits are moderate, the debt ratio will probably stay the same.

However, if debt grows faster than the economy, the ratio will continue to inflate. We are trending in that direction. In the forty-eight years from 1960 to 2008, the ratio increased from 30 to 65 percent. Since 2008, it has almost doubled to 130 percent of GDP, a number most objective economists consider troubling and—to repeat the warnings of the Department of the Treasury—unsustainable. The Ponzi scheme will fail someday.

As noted in the introduction, the balance sheet of the United States has a large negative "net worth" and the liabilities part of the balance sheet doesn't tell the whole story.

The unfunded obligations of Social Security and Medicare (parts A, B, and D), as well as other entitlements, are a major problem, as explained in more detail in chapter 5. The revenue and outlay forecasts indicate a severe shortfall over a seventy-five-year time frame. There is not enough income to cover the payments projected if we continue to pay benefits as they are currently paid. The "present value" of the shortfall is $75.9 trillion, up from a $71 trillion shortfall in 2021. The numbers just keep getting worse. And this only addresses these two programs; none of the other entitlements are included.

The real total liabilities and unfunded obligations as of the fiscal year ending September 30, 2022, are $121.8 trillion, up from $112.0 trillion the prior year—an increase of $9.8 trillion in just one year.

Get the picture yet? Steel yourself and keep reading. It isn't pretty, but we have to understand the problems if we are to address them before the Ponzi scheme fails.

CHAPTER 2

America's Spending Crisis

We should be thankful we are not getting all
the government we are paying for.

—WILL ROGERS

An amazing level of demagoguery surrounds our tax and spending policies. There are sound bites everywhere aimed to arouse emotions in our citizenry—but what are the facts? We need to cut through the meaningless rhetoric and understand the real situation for what it is, not what the politicians scream and holler about.

Consider the following example. In 2017 there was a significant tax reduction. In that year, federal revenue was $3.3 trillion and represented 17.0 percent of the GDP. Jump to 2022, the most recent fiscal year for which the Treasury has published financial reports as of this writing. Revenue was $4.9 trillion and represented 19.2 percent of the GDP. Federal revenue has increased in dollars and as a percentage of GDP since we cut the tax rate. Revenues are now the highest as a percentage of GDP since the Clinton years of the late 1990s (peaking at 19.7 percent) when sound policies also stirred growth.

Federal Receipts as Percentage of Gross Domestic Product

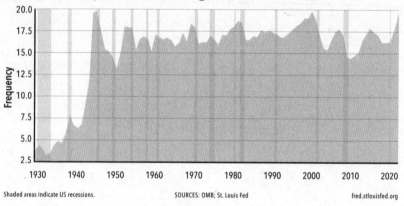

Shaded areas indicate US recessions.   SOURCES: OMB; St. Louis Fed   fred.stlouisfed.org

When was the last time you heard a politician rail about how much tax cuts have cost us? Seems like a daily event. When was the last time you heard them say how they've helped our economy grow? And that the government is still collecting lots of revenue? That's a rare event. Revenues have increased significantly in our growing economy, even though we've had tax cuts—because cutting taxes spurs growth as you will see in later chapters.

You may have heard of the Laffer Curve, named after Arthur Laffer, a modern economist who became famous by explaining that you can get revenue feedback—and maybe in a few cases even increase revenue—by cutting tax rates. Cutting taxes spurs growth, which increases taxable income. There is a point on the curve when the tax rate maximizes tax revenue. If the rate goes lower or higher, revenue decreases. The 2017 tax cuts bear this out, as you can see from the following data. Tax revenue increased from 17.0 percent in 2017 to 19.2 percent of GDP in 2022.

Before the COVID deficit period, spending averaged around 21 percent of GDP. At those levels we would not have the enormous deficits we have today. But spending has not remained at those levels: the spending burden expanded to 24.6 percent of GDP in 2022 and is projected to climb above 25 percent of GDP over the next ten years.

Federal Net Outlays as Percent of Gross Domestic Product

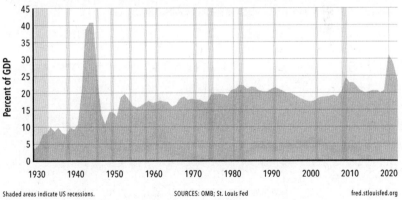

Shaded areas indicate US recessions.   SOURCES: OMB; St. Louis Fed   fred.stlouisfed.org

The Biden budget proposals made in early 2023 would increase taxes by over $5 trillion for the next decade but continue to increase spending by even more. The CBO shows a projected deficit of $20 trillion over this ten-year period. If this policy is followed, it will bring our total interest-bearing debt to over $50 trillion. With that comes an interest expense of approximately $2 trillion, if the average interest rates on all our indebtedness is 4 percent (which is typical of historical interest rates).

Do the math. If we continue to add debt, interest expense eventually becomes the largest part of our budget. We will enter the "doom loop." That is a loop created by large interest payments, leading to higher budget deficits, leading to increasing debt, leading to increasing interest expense, leading to larger deficits ... and the cycle continues. We would never be able to restrain the deficits. CBO projects that spending will reach 30 percent of GDP over the next thirty years if we continue to grow our expenses as projected.

Following is a chart showing past and future projections for the next ten years of revenues and expenses:

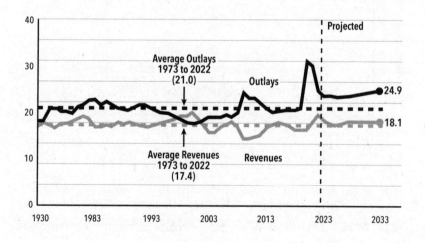

In later chapters we examine the real world and illustrate what policies work for a better economy, and what policies hinder growth.

For now, we will make one generic statement: modest tax rates and spending restraint enable stronger growth. Higher spending, onerous tax rates, larger deficits, and debt financing will slow growth. There is empirical evidence for these statements, which we examine in later chapters. But think about it logically. There is a private sector of the economy, and there is a public sector of the economy. The private sector is the productive part—it produces the goods and services we all consume. The public sector is government, which serves a few necessary functions in a civilized society but otherwise diverts resources from the economy's productive sector. We need capital investment in the private sector to grow our productive capabilities and the economy. If the public sector takes additional capital from the private sector, it reduces the capital available to grow our output. It doesn't matter whether government borrows it to finance the deficit or taxes it away to reduce the deficit, the result is the same: less capital to invest in growing the economy.

Besides borrowing or taxing to fund the public sector, a third choice would be to print money, which the federal government has the power to do. This is not done by physically printing the money; it is done electronically through the Federal Reserve. But creating new money does not increase the output of the economy, so when we create money at a faster rate than we grow the economy, it shows up as inflation, an insidious tax on everyone that harms lower-income folks the most.

So where does this leave us? What is the best policy to pursue for the benefit of all citizens? It seems clear that we need to restrain spending, reduce deficits, and eventually balance the budget.

In theory, there are two choices if we are to get our debts under control. We can significantly raise taxes, hurting the growth of the economy as mentioned above and demonstrated in later chapters. As we've learned from the failure of Europe's welfare states, this approach has a poor track record. Or we can keep taxes as they are and work to control spending with the intention of minimizing and eventually eliminating deficits. If we stop increasing the debt, but grow the economy, over time the debt to GDP ratio will become manageable again. Our path will become sustainable. As you will learn later in the book, this approach has a track record of success.

The best policy choices would focus on restraining spending, not raising taxes. We have become addicted to spending and numb to the borrowing problem. Excessive spending and unsustainable debt do matter—a lot.

Our politicians will not restrain spending unless we, the people, understand and support meaningful change. That is why it is so important to understand what is covered in this book and to support rational changes that can be made for the benefit of the good citizens of this country.

CHAPTER 3

Deficits and Projections

We can't solve our problems with the same
thinking we used when we created them.

—ALBERT EINSTEIN

I t is important to put our data in perspective. In this chapter we present an overview of some historical data and some projections that will highlight the problems. In short, where we are and where we are headed.

The following chart illustrates the history of the federal debt in relation to GDP and the future projections based on data from the CBO, which (by way of a reminder) is a nonpartisan agency of our federal government. This chart shows debt held by the public, which represents the amount of money the federal government has borrowed from private credit markets.

Federal Debt Is on an Unsustainable Path

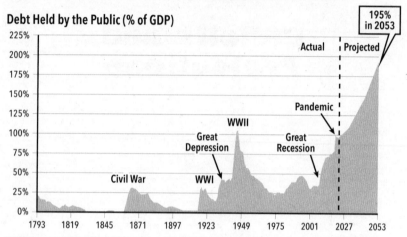

Debt Held by the Public (% of GDP)

SOURCES: Congressional Budget Office, The Budget and Economic Outlook: 2023 to 2033, February 2023; and The Budget and Economic Outlook: 2020 to 2030, January 2020.
© 2023 Peter G. Peterson Foundation

The "gross" debt of the federal government includes the debt "held by the public" along with debt held by various trust funds of the government, mostly Social Security and Medicare Part A. That intragovernmental debt is $6.8 trillion, which makes the following data even worse and brings the total debt as of September 30, 2022, to $31 trillion, about 125 percent of GDP. This is the "debt subject to the debt ceiling cap" that you often hear invoked whenever politicians are debating whether to raise the debt limit. That ceiling is always lifted eventually, but not until politicians have their fun demagoguing each other. If the debt ceiling were not lifted eventually, we would not be able to borrow additional funds to cover the large deficits we continually accrue.

Below is the data since 1962, showing in billions the actual revenues and outlays, alongside budget deficit (-) or surplus.

Revenues, Outlays, Deficits, Surpluses since 1962 Billions of Dollars					
			Deficit (-) or Surplus		
	Revenues	Outlays	On-Budget	Total	Debt Held by the Public
1962	99.7	106.8	-5.9	-7.1	248.0
1963	106.6	111.3	-4.0	-4.8	254.0
1964	112.6	118.5	-6.5	-5.9	256.8
1965	116.8	118.2	-1.6	-1.4	260.8
1966	130.8	134.5	-3.1	-3.7	263.7
1967	148.8	157.5	-12.6	-8.6	266.6
1968	153.0	178.1	-27.7	-25.2	289.5
1969	186.9	183.6	-0.5	3.2	278.1
1970	192.8	195.6	-8.7	-2.8	283.2
1971	187.1	210.2	-26.1	-23.0	303.0
1972	207.3	230.7	-26.1	-23.4	322.4
1973	230.8	245.7	-15.2	-14.9	340.9
1974	263.2	269.4	-7.2	-6.1	343.7
1975	279.1	332.3	-54.1	-53.2	394.7
1976	298.1	371.8	-69.4	-73.7	477.4
1977	355.6	409.2	-49.9	-53.7	549.1
1978	399.6	458.7	-55.4	-59.2	607.1
1979	463.3	504.0	-39.6	-40.7	640.3
1980	517.1	590.9	-73.1	-73.8	711.9

| Revenues, Outlays, Deficits, Surpluses since 1962 Billions of Dollars | | | | |
| | | | Deficit (-) or Surplus | |
	Revenues	Outlays	On-Budget	Total	Debt Held by the Public
1981	599.3	678.2	-73.9	-79.0	789.4
1982	617.8	745.7	-120.6	-128.0	924.6
1983	600.6	808.4	-207.7	-207.8	1,137.3
1984	666.4	851.8	-185.3	-185.4	1,307.0
1985	734.0	946.3	-221.5	-212.3	1,507.3
1986	769.2	990.4	-237.9	-221.2	1,740.6
1987	854.3	1,004.0	-168.4	-149.7	1,889.8
1988	909.2	1,064.4	-192.3	-155.2	2,051.6
1989	991.1	1,143.7	-205.4	-152.6	2,190.7
1990	1,032.0	1,253.0	-277.6	-221.0	2,411.6
1991	1,055.0	1,324.2	-321.4	-269.2	2,689.0
1992	1,091.2	1,381.5	-340.4	-290.3	2,999.7
1993	1,154.3	1,409.4	-300.4	-255.1	3,248.4
1994	1,258.6	1,461.8	-258.8	-203.2	3,433.1
1995	1,351.8	1,515.7	-226.4	-164.0	3,604.4
1996	1,453.1	1,560.5	-174.0	-107.4	3,734.1
1997	1,579.2	1,601.1	-103.2	-21.9	3,772.3
1998	1,721.7	1,652.5	-29.9	69.3	3,721.1
1999	1,827.5	1,701.8	1.9	125.6	3,632.4
2000	2,025.2	1,789.0	86.4	236.2	3,409.8
2001	1,991.1	1,862.8	-32.4	128.2	3,319.6
2002	1,853.1	2,010.9	-317.4	-157.8	3,540.4
2003	1,782.3	2,159.9	-538.4	-377.6	3,913.4
2004	1,880.1	2,292.8	-568.0	-412.7	4,295.5
2005	2,153.6	2,472.0	-493.6	-318.3	4,592.2

Revenues, Outlays, Deficits, Surpluses since 1962 Billions of Dollars			Deficit (-) or Surplus		
	Revenues	Outlays	On-Budget	Total	Debt Held by the Public
2006	2,406.9	2,655.1	-434.5	-248.2	4,829.0
2007	2,568.0	2,728.7	-342.2	-160.7	5,035.1
2008	2,524.0	2,982.5	-641.8	-458.6	5,803.1
2009	2,105.0	3,517.7	-1,549.7	-1,412.7	7,544.7
2010	2,162.7	3,457.1	-1,371.4	-1,294.4	9,018.9
2011	2,303.5	3,603.1	-1,366.8	-1,299.6	10,128.2
2012	2,450.0	3,526.6	-1,138.5	-1,076.6	11,281.1
2013	2,775.1	3,454.9	-719.2	-679.8	11,982.7
2014	3,021.5	3,506.3	-514.3	-484.8	12,779.9
2015	3,249.9	3,691.9	-469.3	-442.0	13,116.7
2016	3,268.0	3,852.6	-620.2	-584.7	14,167.6
2017	3,316.2	3,981.6	-714.9	-665.4	14,665.4
2018	3,329.9	4,109.0	-785.3	-779.1	15,749.6
2019	3,463.4	4,447.0	-991.3	-983.6	16,800.7
2020	3,421.2	6,553.6	-3,142.3	-3,132.4	21,016.7
2021	4,047.1	6,822.4	-2,723.8	-2,775.3	22,284.0
2022	4,896.1	6,271.5	-1,357.5		

The following data represents the CBO's projections for the next ten years.[5]

5 Note that the debt "held by the public" is not our total debt; it does not include debt to other government agencies, such as the IOUs in the Social Security Trust Fund.

	Actual, 2022	2023	2024	2025	2026	2027	2028	2029	2030	2031	2032	2033	Total 2024–2028	Total 2024–2033
In Billions of Dollars														
Revenues														
Individual income taxes	2,632	2,523	2,467	2,511	2,764	3,018	3,121	3,246	3,377	3,515	3,650	3,803	13,881	31,472
Payroll taxes	1,484	1,562	1,633	1,703	1,778	1,849	1,920	1,993	2,068	2,147	2,226	2,307	8,884	19,625
Corporate income taxes	425	475	479	489	495	494	506	514	520	527	527	539	2,462	5,089
Other	356	251	260	264	273	293	369	386	398	414	435	449	1,459	3,540
Total	**4,896**	**4,812**	**4,838**	**4,966**	**5,310**	**5,655**	**5,916**	**6,139**	**6,364**	**6,603**	**6,838**	**7,098**	**26,686**	**59,727**
On-budget	3,830	3,678	3,643	3,711	3,999	4,292	4,501	4,671	4,842	5,023	5,200	5,402	20,145	45,284
Off-budget	1,066	1,133	1,196	1,255	1,311	1,363	1,415	1,468	1,522	1,580	1,637	1,695	6,540	14,443
Outlays														
Mandatory	4,135	3,840	3,812	3,995	4,193	4,395	4,731	4,756	5,115	5,391	5,665	6,140	21,125	48,192
Discretionary	1,662	1,741	1,864	1,955	2,005	2,063	2,119	2,159	2,215	2,266	2,319	2,380	10,007	21,347
Net interest	475	640	739	769	828	903	995	1,071	1,149	1,236	1,333	1,429	4,232	10,451
Total	**6,272**	**6,221**	**6,415**	**6,719**	**7,026**	**7,361**	**7,845**	**7,986**	**8,479**	**8,894**	**9,317**	**9,948**	**35,365**	**79,990**
On-budget	5,188	5,011	5,091	5,297	5,521	5,771	6,163	6,215	6,602	6,908	7,215	7,737	27,843	62,520
Off-budget	1,084	1,210	1,324	1,421	1,504	1,590	1,682	1,771	1,877	1,986	2,102	2,211	7,521	17,470
Total Deficit	**-1,375**	**-1,410**	**-1,576**	**-1,752**	**-1,716**	**-1,706**	**-1,929**	**-1,847**	**-2,115**	**-2,291**	**-2,480**	**-2,851**	**-8,679**	**-20,263**
On-budget	-1,358	-1,333	-1,448	-1,586	-1,523	-1,479	-1,662	-1,544	-1,760	-1,885	-2,015	-2,335	-7,698	-17,236
Off-budget	-18	-77	-129	-166	-193	-227	-266	-303	-355	-407	-465	-516	-981	-3,027
Primary Deficit	-900	-770	-838	-984	-888	-804	-934	-776	-966	-1,055	-1,146	-1,422	-4,447	-9,812
Debt Held by the Public	24,257	25,716	27,370	29,214	30,927	32,645	34,642	36,406	38,604	40,945	43,482	46,445	n.a.	n.a.
Memorandum:														
Gross Domestic Product	25,016	26,238	27,266	28,610	29,932	31,251	32,525	33,811	35,133	36,488	37,874	39,288	149,585	332,179
As a Percentage of Gross Domestic Product														
Revenues														
Individual income taxes	10.5	9.6	9.0	8.8	9.2	9.7	9.6	9.6	9.6	9.6	9.6	9.7	9.3	9.5
Payroll taxes	5.9	6.0	6.0	6.0	5.9	5.9	5.9	5.9	5.9	5.9	5.9	5.9	5.9	5.9
Corporate income taxes	1.7	1.8	1.8	1.7	1.7	1.6	1.6	1.5	1.5	1.4	1.4	1.4	1.6	1.5
Other[a]	1.4	1.0	1.0	0.9	0.9	0.9	1.1	1.1	1.1	1.1	1.1	1.1	1.0	1.1
Total	**19.6**	**18.3**	**17.7**	**17.4**	**17.7**	**18.1**	**18.2**	**18.2**	**18.1**	**18.1**	**18.1**	**18.1**	**17.8**	**18.0**
On-budget	15.3	14.0	13.4	13.0	13.4	13.7	13.8	13.8	13.8	13.8	13.7	13.8	13.5	13.6
Off-budget[b]	4.3	4.3	4.4	4.4	4.4	4.4	4.4	4.3	4.3	4.3	4.3	4.3	4.4	4.3
Outlays														
Mandatory	16.5	14.6	14.0	14.0	14.0	14.1	14.5	14.1	14.6	14.8	15.0	15.6	14.1	14.5
Discretionary	6.6	6.6	6.8	6.8	6.7	6.6	6.5	6.4	6.3	6.2	6.1	6.1	6.7	6.4
Net interest	1.9	2.4	2.7	2.7	2.8	2.9	3.1	3.2	3.3	3.4	3.5	3.6	2.8	3.1
Total	**25.1**	**23.7**	**23.5**	**23.5**	**23.5**	**23.6**	**24.1**	**23.6**	**24.1**	**24.4**	**24.6**	**25.3**	**23.6**	**24.1**
On-budget	20.7	19.1	18.7	18.5	18.4	18.5	18.9	18.4	18.8	18.9	19.0	19.7	18.6	18.8
Off-budget	4.3	4.6	4.9	5.0	5.0	5.1	5.2	5.2	5.3	5.4	5.6	5.6	5.0	5.3
Total Deficit	**-5.5**	**-5.4**	**-5.8**	**-6.1**	**-5.7**	**-5.5**	**-5.9**	**-5.5**	**-6.0**	**-6.3**	**-6.5**	**-7.3**	**-5.8**	**-6.1**
On-budget	-5.4	-5.1	-5.3	-5.5	-5.1	-4.7	-5.1	-4.6	-5.0	-5.2	-5.3	-5.9	-5.1	-5.2
Off-budget	-0.1	-0.3	-0.5	-0.6	-0.6	-0.7	-0.8	-0.9	-1.0	-1.1	-1.2	-1.3	-0.7	-0.9
Primary Deficit	-3.6	-2.9	-3.1	-3.4	-3.0	-2.6	-2.9	-2.3	-2.7	-2.9	-3.0	-3.6	-3.0	-3.0
Debt Held by the Public	97.0	98.0	100.4	102.1	103.3	104.5	106.5	107.7	109.9	112.2	114.8	118.2	n.a.	n.a.

The trends in the preceding table are unambiguously depressing:

Revenue grows 44.9 percent over this period.

Outlays grow 58.6 percent over this period.

Debt grows 92 percent over this period.

"The current fiscal path is unsustainable."

The data reinforces that this is clearly the case. The next step is to look at what is driving the deficits and understand the depth of the problem.

CHAPTER 4

Key Drivers of the Deficits

Economic history is a long record of government policies that failed because they were designed with a bold disregard for the laws of economics.

—LUDWIG VON MISES

We have looked at the data and can now see the problem clearly. So what is the next step? We could bury our heads in the sand and ignore the problem, "kicking the can down the road." Where will that take us? To the end of the Ponzi scheme, when all hell breaks loose. (We will attempt to describe what that could look like in chapter 6.) Or we could sprinkle fairy dust on the problem and hope it disappears. Neither of those options is desirable. We don't believe in magic.

So the next step in our discussion and analysis is to look at the makeup of our revenue and expenses to see what is causing the problem. The following pie charts illustrate the revenue and expenses of the federal government.

Federal Revenue for United States – FY2023

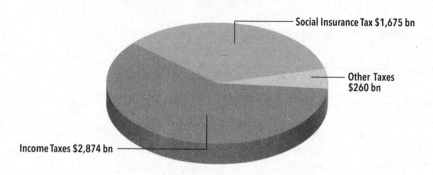

Federal Spending for United States – FY2023

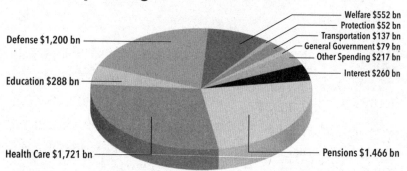

The facts today and for the future are clear. For the fiscal year ending September 30, 2022, federal revenues have increased to record highs both in dollars ($4.8 trillion) and as a percentage of GDP (19.8 percent). However, expenditures are 23.7 percent of GDP and are projected to rise to 30.2 percent over the next ten years. The problem just gets worse.

The federal budget is divided into two main categories: discretionary spending and mandatory spending.

Mandatory Spending

Mandatory spending is "permanently appropriated" by law and generally unlimited in that the programs automatically disburse "such funds as may be necessary." These programs are, in essence, on autopilot. They are not voted on each year unless there are changes proposed to the law, which would of course change the spending. But changes to those programs must be by vote of Congress and signed by the president to change. These programs comprise approximately 70 percent of our spending. The primary items in this category are as follows:

- Social Security
- Medicare
- Medicaid
- Federal Retirement Programs
- Unemployment Compensation
- Student Loans
- Interest Expense
- Agricultural Subsidies

Prior to the enactment of the income tax in 1913, the only nondiscretionary spending was the interest expense—97 percent of spending went through the budgetary process. Now, with 70 percent on autopilot, it requires an act of Congress to change our fiscal trajectory. This is most difficult to do with the partisanship and demagoguery we have today.

Discretionary Spending

This is the spending that Congress "appropriates" each year. It comprises approximately 30 percent of the national budget. The process involves twelve separate appropriations bills. Unfortunately, this is not routinely done as is required, and a continuing resolution (CR) is often passed in its place to fund our government. In either case, differences between the House and Senate are reconciled, and appropriations are sent to the president to sign or veto. If the president signs an appropriation, it becomes the law. If the president vetoes an appropriation, it must go back to Congress to override the veto or change the appropriation to make it acceptable to the president (this sometimes leads to "government shutdown" fights).

The primary items in this category are as follows:
1. Defense
2. Agriculture, Rural Development, Food and Drug Administration, and related agencies
3. Commerce, Justice, Science, and related agencies
4. Energy and Water development
5. Financial Services and general government

6. Homeland Security
7. Interior, Environment, and related agencies
8. Labor, Health and Human Services, Education, and related agencies
9. Legislative branch
10. Military Construction, Veterans Affairs, and related agencies
11. State, Foreign Operations, and related programs
12. Transportation, Housing and Urban Development, and related agencies

Entitlements

Entitlements are the largest drivers of the deficit for many reasons. Social Security, Medicare, and Medicaid are the three big entitlements, but there are many more.

Driving this oversized contribution to the deficit are the demographic trends in our country. We are living longer, with an average life expectancy today of eighty vs. sixty-five when Social Security was first implemented in the 1930s. (Projections are that life expectancy will increase to the mid-eighties or above in the next thirty years.)

However, the retirement age for Social Security has only moved from sixty-five to sixty-seven years old over that period, and early retirement is still at sixty-two—that number has not changed since early retirement became available in 1956. For Medicare, the age of eligibility has been and remains at sixty-five years since its inception in the mid-1960s. With lower birth rates and an aging population, this has changed the ratio of workers to retirees. It was 15 to 1 in the 1950s and higher before that. Today, it is 2.6 to 1 and expected to sink lower in future years. There are not enough workers *pulling* the wagon for the retirees *in* the wagon.

In past years, the fund for Social Security and Medicare Part A did have a positive cash inflow. (Part A is for hospitals and is funded by you and your employer's contributions to the fund.) Now these programs have a negative cash flow, as more is paid out than paid in. The law provides that while the fund lasts, full benefits will be paid as planned. The funds for Social Security will exhaust in 2035 and for Medicare Part A in 2031. At that point, when the fund is exhausted, the current law would require cutting benefits to match revenue. For Social Security, this would be a cut estimated at 22–28 percent. For Medicare Part A, the benefits would be cut an estimated 10 percent.

We have paid into Social Security and Medicare Part A. It is reasonable to believe we are entitled to some return on that investment, but it is a problem when the overall amount of money coming in is much smaller than the amount of money being spent.

Meanwhile, the rest of these entitlements are simply programs put in place by law to pay benefits to various groups. They are not discretionary spending; they are on autopilot unless the law changes. Even Social Security and Medicare Part A are not guaranteed—they work by operation of law.

For Medicare Parts B and D (medical and drugs), the program is voluntary. Those choosing to participate pay a fee, which varies based on income levels. However, the fees only cover 26 percent of the costs; the balance is covered by the general revenues of the country at a cost of over $400 billion per year.

The CBO assumes that the law will be changed to protect benefits on the same level as currently paid for both Social Security and Medicare, all parts. They do not assume any changes to the income of these programs; that is what creates the unfunded obligations in the liability portion of the debt, as illustrated in the debt structure described earlier. Unfunded obligations represent the present value of the revenue shortfall to pay full benefits over a seventy-five-year horizon, given the current income stream. The estimate for unfunded obligations, as of September 30, 2022, is $76 trillion. That is an increase of $5 trillion from the 2021 estimate. This estimate covers only Social Security and Medicare Parts A, B, and D. It does not cover Medicaid. Medicaid is funded solely by general revenues of the government, at a cost of over $500 billion per year.

There are other entitlements, which also drive up the costs. They are much smaller in scale, but they should also be addressed.

Interest Expense

In the short term, it doesn't matter whether capital is taken in the form of taxation or borrowing; the effect to the economy is the same. But in the long term, one consequence of borrowing is that interest payments become a rapidly growing item in the federal budget.

The total interest-bearing debt has increased by $26 trillion in the last twenty years, climbing from $5 trillion to $31 trillion.

The interest expense has been held relatively in check by the artificially low interest rates of the last twelve years. However, that phenomenon has changed rapidly as a result of the large increases in the debt and the return of interest rates to past norms, starting in 2022. Further, there is projected to be a continuing rapid growth of debt. By 2033, it is projected that, following current policy, the debt will be over $50 trillion. If current interest rates (averaging about 4 percent) become the new norm, the interest expense would be $2 trillion per year, the largest single item in the budget.

There are many drivers of excessive spending and deficits, but entitlements and interest payments are the biggest. When we examine the solutions in section III, we will discuss approaches to deal with the overall budget.

The Future

There are some representatives in DC who see the problem we face and are trying to move to more fiscal sanity. There are just not enough of them to get the job done. Even those who realize the problems may not move aggressively enough to move the needle. Some of the recent administrations' budgets are not going to fix the problem. And with the highly partisan alignment of Congress, it is likely nothing would happen even if the White House took the problem seriously.

A big part of the problem is that very few politicians understand that the fundamental problem is that government is growing faster than the economy.

Mitchell's Golden Rule of Economics: growth in government should be slower than growth in the economy. When government grows faster than the economy, Washington spending consumes a larger percent of the GDP. There are plenty of proposals in Washington to further increase the size of government (there are also proposals to increase taxes). Fortunately, few if any of these proposals will make it into law with the divided government we now have. But even if we stop politicians from additional spending, there is already far too much spending in the pipeline.

MITCHELL'S GOLDEN RULE

The Private Sector Should Grow Faster than the Government

The Inflation Reduction Act of 2022 was supposed to increase revenue more than expenses, but it still had a $1.5 trillion deficit. And the proposal did nothing to fix the main drivers of that deficit. It just added more programs and even more taxes. This is still taking capital from the private sector (through taxes and borrowing) and giving it to the government sector.

Wrapping Up

It is not within the scope of this book to detail every driver of the deficit. Our intention is to provide an overview to help you gain awareness of the issues. They must be addressed if we are to ever get back to fiscal sanity and avoid the total collapse of the system in the uncertain future.

In section III, we will address the solutions that are needed to avoid the problems we will face in the future if we do not adopt sound fiscal policy. But first, we need to talk more about entitlements.

CHAPTER 5

Entitlements

Politics is the art of looking for trouble, finding it everywhere,
diagnosing it wrongly, and applying unsuitable remedies.

—ERNEST JOHN PICKSTONE BENN

While there are many policies about spending that can and should be addressed, we single out entitlements as the eight-hundred-pound gorilla in the room. Why? Because entitlements currently make up the single biggest driver of the federal deficit and are the sole cause of the unfunded obligations relating to Social Security and Medicare. (As a reminder, unfunded obligations represent the promises made for future Social Security and Medicare payments for which there is no revenue to cover.)

Fixing this problem does not solve all the financial issues, but it is an essential part of the solution. We must understand the issues and deal with them as soon as possible. The longer we wait, the more difficult the solution will be.

What Are Entitlements?

Entitlements are open-ended obligations of the government to various constituencies for many programs. The spending for these programs is not directly determined by politicians. Instead, spending automatically goes to anyone who satisfies eligibility criteria (usually based on age or income). These programs are on autopilot. To change them requires new legislation that gets approved by Congress and then signed by the president.

The three major programs we will focus on are Social Security, Medicare, and Medicaid. These are the largest drivers of entitlement spending. Medicare is separated into three parts: Part A is for hospitals; Part B is for medical; Part D is for drugs. We need to understand some of the facts about these programs and why they are critical. Once we understand the problems, we will be amenable to reasonable changes to make them sustainable.

Social Security/Disability

This program began during the Great Depression to benefit retirees and the disabled. A tax was levied on the employee and matched by the employer to fund the programs. These taxes were paid into a trust fund. Since there were many working relative to the number of those retired, the trust fund grew.

As we've mentioned, workers initially became eligible for Social Security with a reduced benefit option at sixty-two with the full benefit option beginning at sixty-five. Today, the eligibility age for full benefits is more than sixty-six years old and soon will rise to sixty-seven (but it is still sixty-two for reduced benefits). In the beginning, there were up to thirty people working to support each retiree so the system was financially sound. Today, as a result of demographic changes, there are only 2.6 people working to support each retiree. This has resulted in a deficit each year; the income from taxes simply does not cover the benefits that are paid out.

The Social Security Trust Fund is largely a bookkeeping fiction, but it is real in one sense. When the IOUs in the trust fund are depleted in just a few years, benefits must be cut so that the benefits equal income. That will require an estimated 20–28 percent cut in benefits given the facts we know today.

Medicare, Hospitalization (Part A)

Medicare was started in the 1960s to provide medical insurance for Americans when they turn sixty-five years old. Part A, hospitalization, is partly funded by a tax on employees, matched by their employers. Another trust fund was created. The eligibility age of sixty-five has remained the same since the program's inception. The insurance covers 80 percent of eligible costs (an individual could buy private supplemental insurance to cover the rest if they chose to). Once again, as a result of demographic changes, the income from the tax no longer covers the benefits paid. The fund will be depleted in 2031. The law provides that when that happens, benefits must be cut to equal income. That will require a 10 percent cut in benefits based on current estimates.

Medicare, Medical and Drugs (Part B and Part D)

These two programs provide optional, fee-based coverage for medical and drug expenses. Individuals become eligible when they reach sixty-five years old. There are no taxes or funds to cover them; the income for these programs comes only from user fees, and the shortfall is paid by the general revenues of the government. User fees cover about 26 percent of the benefits; the other 74 percent comes from general revenue (i.e., taxpayers).

Medicaid

This program was also begun in the 1960s to provide medical care for those low-income people who could not afford insurance. Eligibility is based on income.

This is a program that is funded totally by the general revenues of the federal government and the states; there are no dedicated taxes or user fees. Approximately 65 percent of the costs are paid by the federal government.

Here is a summary of these entitlement programs' revenue and expenses for the year ending September 30, 2022:

(In Billions)	Revenue	Expenses	Deficit
Social Security/Disability	$1,007	$1,135	$128
Medicare Part A (hospital)	$330	$332	$2

Medicare Parts B and D (medical/drugs)	$144	$511	$367
Medicaid	$0	$519	$519
Total	$1,481	$2,497	$1,016

This is the annual deficit for one year: $1.016 trillion for just these three entitlement programs (there are others).

The CBO releases an annual projection of what the unfunded obligations for Social Security and Medicare would be (Medicaid is not projected as an unfunded obligation) if we continue to pay benefits as promised under today's law (without the automatic cuts the law provides). The value of the shortfall was $76-plus trillion in 2022. Politicians do not want to lower benefits for retirees. Maintaining them will require a change in the law. Under the assumption that they will do just that, the federal deficit and debt stand to grow even faster.

Future Projections

The problems get worse from here. The demographic trends and costs of these programs are increasing. In 2022, Social Security spent $1.2 trillion, about 21 percent of all federal expenditures. In 2033, with no changes, it is projected to spend $2.3 trillion, about 24 percent of federal expenditures, and the trust fund will be exhausted. With no changes, all programs just get more expensive.

What This Means to You

For most of our contemporaries and for all future generations, the funds for Social Security and Medicare Part A will be depleted if the programs are not changed. Either benefits will be cut or, if they continue to be paid, there will be significant additional federal deficits and debt or significant increases in taxes for everyone. Probably both. The large deficits in Medicare Parts B and D will continue to grow. This is not workable. These problems must be addressed.

Almost all of our politicians pander to the public by saying they will not touch Social Security and Medicare because that is what they perceive we want. They may be right. That is why it is so important for the voting public to understand the problem and agree that it must be fixed. It can be fixed without savaging current retirees—but it will not be without some costs. Until the public understands that these programs must be touched if we are ever to reach fiscal sanity, the politicians will not change them (until a disaster forces them to come to grips with the issue). However, the longer we wait, the more difficult the changes will be to make, with much more economic pain to sustain them.

As noted, we will deal with some ideas on fixing these programs in section III, but the complexity is beyond the scope of this book to address in full. A commission will need to study this problem in-depth and develop practical solutions.

CHAPTER 6

What Happens If . . .

We are now entering the twilight zone, the world of the future. What follows is sheer conjecture, a product of our understanding of economics and our imaginations. What might happen if we do not get our house in order and if the world doesn't stop buying the fiction that the federal government can repay the trillions of dollars it has borrowed?

We'll start with good news. This grim fantasy will never occur *if* we get our fiscal house in order by restraining spending. That approach will reduce the debt as a percentage of GDP, especially if Washington can maintain a sane fiscal policy.

The bad news is that this dystopian fantasy, or some semblance of it, will occur if we stay on the present course. In ten years, the burden of government spending will be much higher, and the interest-bearing debt will be over $50 trillion—with around $2 trillion of interest (using historical interest rate average of 4 percent). We will then enter the doom loop, with growing debt and interest costs compounding, leaving us unable to ever balance a budget until . . .

The Setup

Somewhere in the future, our interest-bearing debt has risen to $75 trillion. The world is aware of the risk of default on that debt, and the interest rate has risen to 8 percent to reflect that risk. Our interest cost is $6 trillion per year. Social Security and Medicare trusts have long been exhausted, yet we continue to pay out benefits as always. The deficit is in the multitrillion-dollar level every year, and there is seemingly no way to balance it or get it back to near balance. We have become addicted to excessive spending and debt financing. We have taxed the rich to the point that they are disincentivized to produce, compounding our economic problem by stopping growth.

We have done the unthinkable: we have managed to drive this country, once the greatest tower of financial strength and prosperity in the world, into bankruptcy. No one will buy our debt. And as our old debt matures, we cannot sell new debt to refinance it, so we have the compound problem of paying $6 trillion in interest and being forced to pay off existing debt as it matures. About $12 trillion of debt matures each year, so we must add $18 trillion to keep the country from defaulting.

The math does not work, even if you assume our economy has grown to $50 trillion GDP and our tax revenues have risen to a record-high of 25 percent of GDP, or $12.5 trillion.

We are bankrupt.

What Now?

Scenario 1: Print Money

The first scenario that comes up is just to print the money, figuratively speaking. The Federal Reserve, America's central bank, has the ability to create more money. Would the Fed do something irresponsible? Well, our total cost of government will have increased to 30 percent of GDP ($15 trillion), so the cost of operating the country, with a net interest expense of $6 trillion, is $9 trillion. To pay the interest and principal of $18 trillion plus $9 trillion to operate, we need to print $27 trillion to cover all the cash needs of the federal government.

We fire up the printing press, sort of like Argentina, and enter an inflation spiral from which there is no escape. Money loses its value, and the normal markets grind to a halt. Barter becomes a primary form of exchange. Poverty and food insecurity become rampant. Desperate people do desperate things, and crime waves evolve. Law and order break down slowly at first, then escalate out of control. Civilized society as we know it grinds to a standstill. Chaos ensues, every person for himself. Survival of the fittest, the folks with the biggest clubs, win.

The politicians initially try to fix the unfixable. The outrageous debts have accumulated over many years of fiscal irresponsibility. There is no way out. Two hundred and fifty years of progress wiped out by irresponsible government.

This seems unimaginable, but peek at a real-world example—Venezuela. In the course of fifteen to twenty years, Venezuela turned one of the soundest economies in South America into a basket case. Inflation reached 1 million percent for a time. There was a 50 percent poverty rate, so many millions voted with their feet and fled to other countries. A true revolution requires arms, and the government disarmed the public long ago. The only people who had arms were the military and police, both loyal to the government—the hand that fed them.

For those who are concerned about inequality, look at the results in Venezuela. The rulers and their chosen henchmen are just fine, and the rest of the country is in shambles, unable to get adequate food and shelter.

Will this happen to the US? Probably not the same way it happened in Venezuela, but we are on the road to financial ruin. We may be traveling down a different path, but the results could be just as devastating.

Scenario 2: Default on the Debt

In a less severe economic scenario, we might use our taxes to pay the interest and honor the debt. We would simply run the government on what was left, forcing draconian cuts to everything, including entitlements, since the funds would simply not be available to honor all the commitments. That would lead to some sort of crisis. However, it is not an option in the setup just described—the total tax income ($12.5 trillion) is not enough to pay the interest and maturing debt ($18 trillion).

The only remaining option is to default on the debt—just stop paying interest and stop repaying maturing debt.

When we default, $75 trillion of assets held by the public, institutions, and governments around the world plunge in value. The value of US government debt may even become worthless. Investors in government debt would not get the interest that they expected. Many financial institutions around the world would fail, and a banking panic would ensue, causing a total financial collapse around the world. There would be no workable monetary system, as most of the money supply is in the form of credits at the banks, not physical currency. Mass deflation would occur, as there would be little demand for anything in the absence of a functional monetary system. Barter would (again) become the main form of economic exchange. Desperation would follow. Law and order would break down. The thugs with the biggest clubs would prevail. We would be barbarians again.

Summary

Is any of this possible? Will this doomsday scenario actually happen? We would like to say this is impossible, and we hope and pray we never come close to these possibilities. However, we are on the trail to an outcome that will eventually be disastrous.

Will it be as apocalyptic as described? Probably not. But as we have seen in Venezuela, big government means ruinous taxes, disastrous deficits, and reckless money printing, plus policies that disincentivize productive work. It can all combine in a short time to destroy centuries of progress.

In the prior chapters we discussed the issues in some detail. The Department of the Treasury has stated for many years that we are on a path that is fiscally unsustainable. Our projected interest-bearing debt in ten years will be over $50 trillion. Social Security and Medicare trust funds will be exhausted. Deficits and debt will continue to mount. Where will it end?

Winston Churchill famously quipped, "Americans always do the right thing, once all other alternatives are exhausted."

When we finally get around to doing the right thing, will it be too late?

Real-World Fiscal Lessons

Overview

Taxpayers in the United States often complain about wasteful, excessive, and inefficient government, and there is plenty of evidence to justify their anger. But Americans are lucky compared to Europeans. We have a medium-sized welfare state with a relatively high tax burden. Looking at the other side of the Atlantic, by contrast, European nations generally have large-sized welfare states with a very high tax burden.

If we look on the other side of the Pacific, however, we can find some very different comparisons. There are a handful of "tiger" economies, such as Singapore, Taiwan, and Hong Kong, that have relatively small governments with small-sized welfare states and relatively low tax burdens.

If you look at the overall burden of government spending in developed nations, the United States is in the middle. As shown in the following chart, we have small government compared to nations such as Italy and France. But we have big government compared to countries such as Singapore and Taiwan.

Major Differences in the Burden of Govenrment Spending

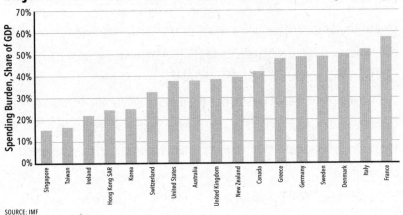

SOURCE: IMF

75

Notice that all these jurisdictions are developed nations (even Greece presumably qualifies). The countries in the chart are what used to be called "first world nations," part of the industrialized world. They all have the things that most people expect and want from government such as decent infrastructure, universal education, and accessible health care.

Yet why is it that some nations get those things at much lower cost? The burden of government in the United States (consuming nearly 38 percent of economic output) is more than twice the level of Singapore and Taiwan (where government consumes about 16 percent of GDP). Are American taxpayers getting two times as much value as the people in Singapore and Taiwan? The answer is definitely no.

Or think about the unfortunate taxpayers of France and Italy. They have a burden of government spending (more than 50 percent of GDP) that is more than three times larger than what people deal with in Singapore and Taiwan. Are the French and Italians getting three times as much value from government? The answer is not just no, it is laughably no.

But we should not focus solely on what people are getting from government. We also want to consider whether some governments are so big that they stifle economic growth. As noted elsewhere in the book, there are several things that determine a country's prosperity—whether measured by overall level of prosperity (per capita GDP) or by annual growth (changes in GDP)—and fiscal policy is definitely one of the main factors.

It is no coincidence that some of the nations with relatively small governments, such as Singapore and Taiwan, have very impressive track records. They tend to enjoy rapid growth, and they also enjoy high living standards. Indeed, as shown in the following chart, Singapore has even surpassed the United States in per capita GDP. And Taiwan is now more prosperous than France and Italy.

Singapore Surpasses the United States, Taiwain Passes France and Italy

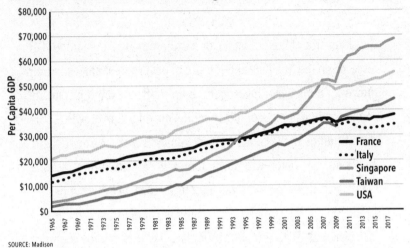

SOURCE: Madison

So why have Italy and France languished? Not everything depends on fiscal policy, to be sure, but it is highly likely that those two nations suffer from weak economic performance in part because they have heavy fiscal burdens. Too much of their economy's output is being diverted to politicians—who tend to spend money unwisely—and the high tax burdens that accompany all that spending further discourage economic activity.

Let us now shift from case studies to scholarly evidence. There are hundreds of academic studies we could cite, but we assume that would be tedious and boring for readers. Moreover, skeptical readers might wonder if we are selectively citing the work of only market-friendly economists. So we have decided to focus on research from international bureaucracies that have left-leaning reputations. We will start with some research from Jean-Marc Fournier and Åsa Johansson at the Paris-based Organisation for Economic Co-operation and Development. Their 2016 study, "The Effect of the Size and the Mix of Public Spending on Growth and Inequality," determined that large governments undermine prosperity:

> The sheer size of the public sector has prompted a large amount of research on the link between the size of government and economic growth. . . . This paper investigates empirically the effect of the size and the composition of public spending on long-term growth. . . . The main findings that emerge from the analysis are ... Larger governments are associated with lower long-term growth. Larger governments also slow down the catch-up to the productivity frontier. . . . a reduction in the size of the government could increase long-term GDP by about 10 percent, with much larger effects in some countries with currently large or ineffective governments.[6]

Next, we will look at some research from the World Bank. In a 2012 report titled *Golden Growth: Restoring the Lustre of the European Economic Model*, Indermit Singh Gill and Martin Raiser look at the relationship between fiscal policy and national prosperity. Once again, the results show that government should be much smaller.

> We provide new econometric evidence on the impact of government size on growth using a panel of advanced and emerging economies since 1995. . . . They suggest that a 10 percentage point increase in initial government spending as a share of GDP in Europe is associated with a reduction in annual real per capita GDP growth of around 0.6–0.9 percentage points a year. . . . The regression results

6 https://www.oecd.org/economy/public-finance/The-effect-of-the-size-and-the-mix-of-public-spending-on-growth-and-inequality-working-paper.pdf.

for Europe, using the same approach as outlined earlier, show a consistently negative effect of social transfers on growth.[7]

These are powerful results. Bigger government means less growth. And the effect is especially clear when measuring the impact of social transfers (the welfare state) on economic performance. Here is a chart from the study, showing that bigger governments are associated with less prosperity when looking at all countries. And the relationship is very strong when looking at European nations.

Growth Is Slower as Government Gets Bigger
(median growth by average government size, percent, 1995-2010)

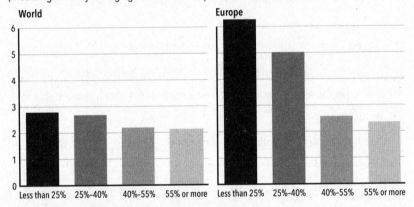

NOTE:The horizontal axis shows government spending as a percentage of GDP.
Source: World Bank staff calculations, based on Eurostat, IMF WEO, OECD National Accounts Statistics, and WDI.

Now it is time to review some research from the European Central Bank. A 2013 study by António Afonso and João Tovar Jalles titled "Fiscal Composition

7   Indermit Singh Gill and Martin Raiser, *Golden Growth: Restoring the Lustre of the European Economic Model* (Washington, DC: World Bank Publications, 2012), https://documents1.worldbank.org/curated/en/539371468036253854/pdf/Main-report.pdf.

and Long-Term Growth" found a significantly negative relationship between government spending and economic growth. Here is a key excerpt from the report:

> In this study we use a large panel of developed and developing countries for the period 1970–2008. ... Specifically, we examine the following issues: the influence of which budgetary components have a stronger influence in affecting (positively or negatively) per capita GDP growth rates. ... Our evidence suggests that for the full sample. ... government expenditures appear with significant negative signs. ... public wages, interest payments, subsidies and government consumption have a negative effect on output growth.[8]

Based on these studies, as well as the examples cited at the beginning of this section, it is clear that big government has a very negative effect on economic performance. That is true elsewhere in the world, and it is true in the United States.

In the chapters that follow, we will review examples of countries that do well and some of the key information about their economies, countries that do poorly and their key information, and the history of some good and bad economic eras in the United States. In the final chapter we will wrap up by using this real-world data to draw conclusions about the key factors that affect the prosperity of a nation.

8 https://www.ecb.europa.eu/pub/pdf/scpwps/ecbwp1518.pdf.

CHAPTER 7

Failing Countries

The lesson of this section is very simple and straightforward: bad things happen when government is too big and grows too fast. Indeed, all the markers of bad fiscal policy, such as high deficits, economic weakness, government waste, and excessive taxation, are almost always caused by too much spending.

Not everyone agrees, however, on what it means for government to be "too big." There is not a consensus on the right way to measure if and when government is growing "too fast." Readers will have to use their own judgment, but the CBO and OECD research cited in the introduction to this section indicate that many European nations have spending burdens that are far too onerous. The burden of government spending in the United States has reached worrisome levels as well.

Let's start this section with a bit of history. Nations in the developed world used to have very small governments. The burden of federal government spending in the United States was trivially small throughout the 1800s and into the early 1900s. The same was true in other advanced nations as well.

Here is some data from a 2000 book by two economists who used to work for the International Monetary Fund.[9] As you can see, there was a rather modest burden of government spending in the world's richest nations (smaller than the size of government today in places such as Singapore and Taiwan).

Growth of General Government Expenditure, (Percentage of GDP)

	Late 19th Century about 1870	1913
General government for all years		
Australia	18.3	16.5
Austria	10.5	17.0
Canada	...	...
France	12.6	17.0
Germany	10.0	14.8
Italy	13.7	17.1
Ireland	...	...
Japan	8.8	8.3
New Zealand	...	...
Norway	5.9	9.3
Sweden	5.7	10.4
Switzerland	16.5	14.0
United Kingdom	9.4	12.7
Average	**10.8**	**13.1**

9   Ludger Schuknecht and Vito Tanzi, *Public Spending in the 20th Century: A Global Perspective* (Cambridge: Cambridge University Press, 2000).

What's the size of government today? Let's look at the same table, but let's add the latest numbers for 2023 based on the IMF's World Economic Outlook database. We don't know if the methodology used to calculate these numbers is the same, and we should also assume that the estimates for 1870 and 1913 are probably not very precise. But even with those caveats, we can confidently conclude that the burden of government spending has exploded over the past 110 years. Government is now consuming more than three times as much of economic output in 2023 as it did in 1913.

Growth of General Government Expenditure,
(Percentage of GDP)

	Late 19th Century about 1870	1913	2023
General government for all years			
Australia	18.3	16.5	37.8
Austria	10.5	17.0	50.8
Canada	...	...	...
France	12.6	17.0	57.7
Germany	10.0	14.8	48.7
Italy	13.7	17.1	52.2
Ireland	...	...	...
Japan	8.8	8.3	38.8
New Zealand	...	...	...
Norway	5.9	9.3	45.5
Sweden	5.7	10.4	48.8
Switzerland	16.5	14.0	32.7
United Kingdom	9.4	12.7	38.5
United States	7.3	7.5	37.7
Average	**10.8**	**13.1**	**44.5**

The reason government used to be very small and is now much bigger is the welfare state. It did not begin until the German government imposed a version of Social Security in the 1880s. But that program was very modest, at least compared to such expenditures today. If we go back a hundred years into the past, we find that only a tiny share of economic output was used for either social insurance or income redistribution. Here is a chart from the *Our World in Data* site from Oxford University. As you can see, "public social spending" barely existed prior to the 1930s and did not became a major fiscal burden in most nations until after 1960.

As noted, opinions differ on when government is too big or growing too fast. But it is easy to understand whether and why

Public Social Spending as a Share of GDP, 1880 to 2016

Social spending includes, among others, the following areas: health, old age, incapacity-related benefits, family, active labor market programs, unemployment, and housing.

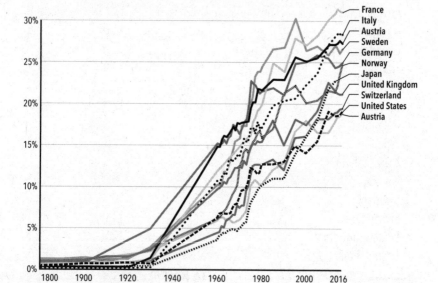

Source: Our World in Data based on OECD and Lindert (2004)
OurWorldInData.org/government-spending • CCBY

government is growing. The preceding chart clearly shows that governments have become a much bigger burden on GDP, especially in regard to expenditures for the welfare state. The rest of this section examines various nations to see if we can determine a relationship between government spending, fiscal problems, and the impact on an economy.

We will start by looking at two examples of fiscal collapse: Greece and Argentina. Those nations have received a lot of attention, so understanding their problems is important. That will be followed by a look at other nations that have required bailouts and have not received as much media coverage of what went wrong, so we will try to fill the gap. Then we will wrap up this portion of the book with a look at a couple of nations that are heading toward fiscal crisis, followed by a discussion of some of the world's worst economies.

Major Disasters

It is entirely subjective to classify nations as major disasters or minor disasters. This section will consider the examples of Greece and Argentina. These nations are considered major disasters because they received very large bailouts and got lots of media coverage.

Greece

Back in 2009, Greece went through a major economic and fiscal crisis and was repeatedly bailed out by the European Commission, the European Central Bank, and the International Monetary Fund.

Its economy fell into a deep depression, rivaling America's Great Depression of the 1930s. Today, nearly fifteen years after the crisis, living standards are not even close to recovering.

What caused this crisis? The simple answer is that Greek government debt had climbed to record levels, equal to more than 100 percent of Greek economic output, and investors suddenly became fearful that the Greek government was on an unsustainable trajectory. The only way Greece could pay for the deficits and maturing bonds was to borrow more money. And when the investors who bought government bonds decided the Greek government could not be trusted to pay off maturing bonds and the interest on those bonds, they stopped buying the bonds. There was then no longer any ability to engage in deficit spending, leading to a fiscal crisis.

That simple answer is correct, but not complete. Because the real cause of the crisis was a dramatic increase in the burden of government spending, resulting in increasing fiscal deficits. This

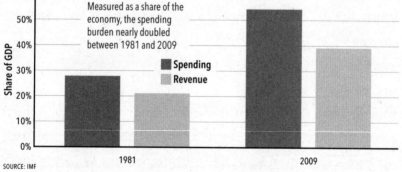

Greece: Big Tax Increase, but Bigger Spending Increase

Measured as a share of the economy, the spending burden nearly doubled between 1981 and 2009

■ Spending
■ Revenue

Share of GDP

SOURCE: IMF

chart shows what happened to Greek taxes and spending between 1981 and 2009, measured as a share of gross domestic product. Government nearly doubled in size.

In other words, taxes increased significantly, but because the spending burden grew much faster, there was an ever-increasing amount of government debt. But the debt was merely a symptom. The underlying disease was excessive government spending. The tax increases simply made a bad situation even worse. Higher tax burdens stifled the private sector by taking capital from the producers. And the higher spending also undermined growth by enabling more Greek citizens to become dependent on government largesse.

Another way to show the fiscal mess in Greece is to contrast the growth of government to the growth of the private sector. As you can see from this chart, the government's budget grew more than twice as fast as the private economy. Given these horrifying numbers, it's a surprise that the fiscal crisis did not occur even sooner.

Greek Crisis Caused by Excessive Spending Growth

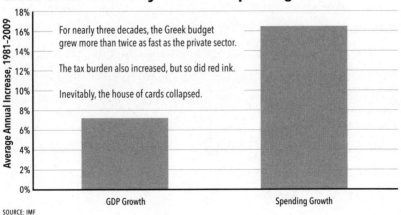

For nearly three decades, the Greek budget grew more than twice as fast as the private sector.

The tax burden also increased, but so did red ink.

Inevitably, the house of cards collapsed.

GDP Growth

Spending Growth

SOURCE: IMF

Let's close by examining the impact of the Greek bailout. Since investors would not buy Greek bonds, the EU and other bureaucracies had to bail Greece out by providing funds. The good news is that Greece was forced to engage in some long-overdue spending restraint; the burden of government spending has now been reduced when measured as a share of GDP. The bad news is that the tax burden increased, making it harder for the private sector economy to recover. The final insult to injury is that Greece has even more debt today than when the crisis began in 2009.

Argentina

Argentina is a poster child for bad fiscal policy. According to Professor Steve Hanke of Johns Hopkins University, it has received more than twenty IMF bailouts. A bailout is required when a country is insolvent, and no investors will buy its debt. As with all nations that get into fiscal trouble, politicians in Argentina cannot resist increasing spending at an unsustainable rate. To make matters worse, the government likes to use monetary policy (printing money) as a means of financing its bloated budget.

The net result, as seen in the following chart, is that Argentina has an inflation problem as well as a spending problem. But it also has a tax problem and a debt problem. No matter how you slice the data, Argentina is a mess. The failure to control spending with their economic policies has meant a combination of higher taxes, higher debt, and higher inflation. This is what led to the IMF bailouts to help pay Argentina's obligations.

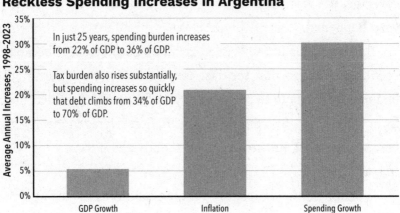

Reckless Spending Increases in Argentina

In just 25 years, spending burden increases from 22% of GDP to 36% of GDP.

Tax burden also rises substantially, but spending increases so quickly that debt climbs from 34% of GDP to 70% of GDP.

SOURCE: IMF

Unfortunately, the various IMF bailouts have not been successful. Taxes go up, but spending goes up even more. The sad history of Argentina is that significant portions of the extra spending are financed with red ink and money printing.

Minor Disasters

Let's also look at some secondary examples. Most of these nations have suffered fiscal crises in recent years. How did they get in trouble? Looking at the data, we see some common themes.

Lebanon

There is nothing "minor" about the disaster in Lebanon. The meltdown started in 2021, and the nation is still in crisis. Nobody knows the final economic and fiscal cost, but the aggregate damage easily could exceed what happened in Greece and Argentina. But since Lebanon is a small nation that does not attract much media coverage, the vast majority of people are totally unfamiliar with what happened.

This chart fills in the blanks. Lebanon got in trouble because spending was growing too fast for too long. The government budget rose by about 18 percent per year for nearly three decades, from 1991–2018. By comparison, inflation averaged nearly 10 percent, and GDP growth averaged slightly above 10 percent over the same period.

Lebanon got in trouble by spending too much for too long; it will be instructive to investigate what would have happened if the government had been constrained by a spending cap. This next chart was put together in 2018 to show that the country would not have suffered a fiscal crisis if spending had been limited to growth of 6 percent per year.

Nearly Three Decades of Excessive Spending Growth in Lebanon

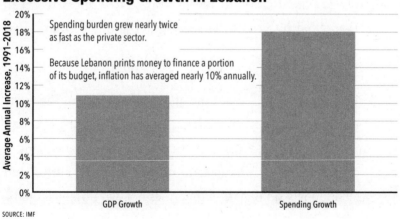

Spending burden grew nearly twice as fast as the private sector.

Because Lebanon prints money to finance a portion of its budget, inflation has averaged nearly 10% annually.

SOURCE: IMF

A 6 Percent Spending Cap

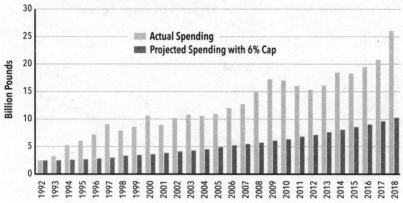

Lebanon isn't just a case study of excessive spending. The country also shows the danger of financing a budget by printing money. Some people call that approach "modern monetary theory" (the belief that government can finance its spending by printing money), but the name doesn't matter. What's important is that it is extraordinarily foolish to compound the damage of bad fiscal policy with bad monetary policy. As we have learned, when the money supply grows faster than economic output, the result is inflation.

Pakistan

There was a fiscal crisis in Pakistan in 2019, and the IMF came in with a bailout. Sadly, the IMF focused on increasing the nation's tax burden. That choice was especially puzzling since the IMF's own data showed that Pakistan was a lot like Greece. Revenues increased significantly in the year before the crisis. The nation got in trouble because the spending burden increased even faster.

Where's the Austerity in Pakistan?
Government Spending Has Tripled in Real Terms

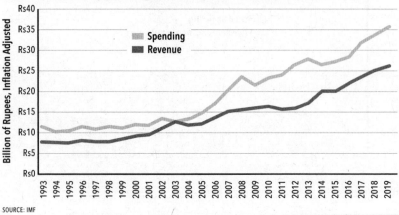

SOURCE: IMF

This chart shows what happened both to revenues and spending over a twenty-five-year period, adjusted for inflation. The obvious takeaway is that spending grew too fast for too long. Pakistan did not have a problem of declining tax revenue.

Incidentally, if Lebanon was an example of how modern monetary theory makes fiscal policy even worse, Pakistan is an example of how bailouts make fiscal policy even worse. The nation has been "rescued" by the IMF more than twenty times according to Professor Steve Hanke of Johns Hopkins University. The net effect of all those bailouts seems to be more spending, more taxes, and more debt.

Cyprus

Back in 2013, Cyprus suffered a fiscal crisis and had to get bailed out by the IMF. Some said Cyprus was dealing with inadequate revenues, but the tax burden between 1996 and 2011 jumped from 29 percent of GDP to nearly 37 percent, according to the IMF. The problem with Cyprus, as shown by the following chart, is that spending grew even faster, rising from 30 percent to 42 percent of GDP.

Cyprus Spends into a Fiscal Crisis

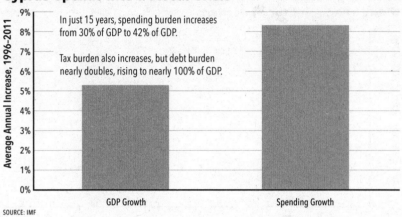

In just 15 years, spending burden increases from 30% of GDP to 42% of GDP.

Tax burden also increases, but debt burden nearly doubles, rising to nearly 100% of GDP.

SOURCE: IMF

As we have repeatedly noted, nations get in trouble when there is an extended period of government growing faster than the private sector. That is also depicted in this chart. As is generally the case, there were other factors contributing to the economic and debt crises. In the case of Cyprus, the banking sector was poorly managed. That led to a bailout. But a weak banking sector would not have produced a crisis if Cyprus had a strong record of spending restraint.

Jordan

Another country that got a bailout last decade is Jordan. As readers might suspect, the country got in trouble because politicians allowed spending to grow too fast. In the case of Jordan, the numbers are extraordinary. Over a fifteen-year period, as shown in the chart, average annual spending increases were three times larger than annual increases in the private sector.

Spending Burden Grows Three Times Faster than Private Sector in Jordan

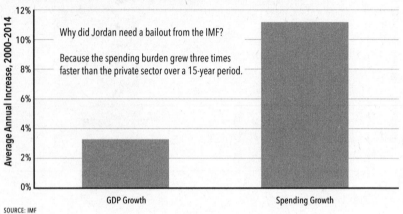

Why did Jordan need a bailout from the IMF?

Because the spending burden grew three times faster than the private sector over a 15-year period.

SOURCE: IMF

That's a terrible approach for one or two years. When it happens for fifteen years, it's a recipe for fiscal and economic crisis. Which is exactly what happened in Jordan. And since the IMF has a bad habit of pushing for tax increases when giving bailouts (thus weakening growth and enabling more future spending, resulting in larger deficits), it's very likely that there will be more bailouts in Jordan's future.

Predicting a Fiscal Crisis

Is there a way of predicting which nations will suffer a fiscal crisis at some point in the not-too-distant future? The International Monetary Fund produced a study on this topic.[10] It warned that several bad policy choices can help set the stage for economic problems. The study specifically warns about "the pace of expansion in public expenditures" and "high expenditure growth." The bottom line, according to the authors, is that "rising public expenditures increase the probability of a crisis." With that warning in mind, let's look at two countries that may soon get in trouble.

Italy

Like many European nations, Italy dramatically increased the burden of government spending after World War II. Politicians expanded the welfare state, especially after the enactment of a value-added tax, which was a money machine for bigger government. By the end of the 1980s, government spending was consuming half of the nation's economic output, and government debt was approaching 100 percent of GDP.

That's the bad news. However, in recent decades the government has slowed spending increases. Indeed, the spending burden has grown by an average of only 3.7 percent annually over past twenty-five years. Unfortunately, as shown in the following

10 Cerovic, Svetlana et al, "Predicting Fiscal Crises," IMF Working Paper No. 18/181, August 2018, https://ssrn.com/abstract=3236796.

chart, the private economy is growing at a slower rate, which adds to Italy's problems.

The net result is that Italy has an enormous fiscal burden. Spending is excessive, taxes are excessive, and debt is excessive. But Italy does not have its own currency, so Italian politicians don't have the ability to finance spending by printing money. The European Central Bank is making that mistake by providing funding, as Italy is not able to sell its bonds. The EU is basically printing money.

There is no easy way of predicting if and when Italy will suffer a fiscal/debt crisis, particularly since the European Central Bank has been engaged in an indirect bailout by buying up lots of Italian debt. But it may just be a matter of time before the house of cards comes tumbling down. Disaster will strike when they cannot sell their bonds to the public, and the European Central Bank stops buying them.

Italy's Fiscal Erosion

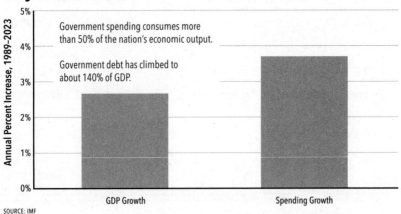

Government spending consumes more than 50% of the nation's economic output.

Government debt has climbed to about 140% of GDP.

SOURCE: IMF

South Africa

Another nation that may be stumbling toward a fiscal crisis is South Africa. Over the past two-plus decades, the burden of government has grown at nearly twice the rate as the economy's productive sector. As a result of excessive spending growth, the South African government is now consuming 33 percent of economic out put, up sharply from 22 percent at the turn of the century.

**Spending Burden in South Africa
Growing Nearly Twice as Fast as Economy**

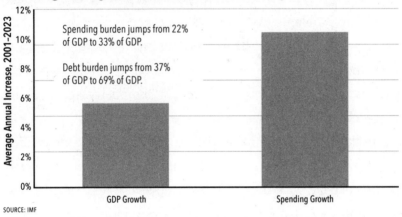

SOURCE: IMF

One consequence of ever-increasing spending is ever-increasing debt. According to the IMF, the debt burden has nearly doubled since 2001, climbing from 37 percent of economic output to 69 percent of economic output. This is much lower than Italian debt, but investors (the people who buy and sell government bonds) tend to be more leery of high levels of debt from poorer nations.

We can assume that the burden of government spending will continue to grow rapidly, but there is time for South Africa to turn policy in the other direction (the same is true for Italy). But if that does not happen, do not be surprised if South Africa has a fiscal crisis in the next few years.

Disaster Economies

The world has some very poor nations. Countries such as North Korea, Cuba, Democratic Republic of the Congo, Venezuela, Sudan, Haiti, and Yemen have grinding poverty and massive economic problems. As a general rule, these nations have bad fiscal policy. However, their problems go way beyond high tax rates and wasteful spending. Indeed, it is safe to say that problems such as rule of law, corruption, and lack of property rights are the biggest barriers to prosperity in these countries.

In the case of communist nations, the damage is compounded by the absence of many economic signals. The government controls what gets built, what investments occur, what wages are paid, and what prices are charged. The rest of the world learned a long time ago that such policies are a recipe for failure. Simply stated, the clunky top-down policies in a command-and-control economy are grotesquely inefficient compared to the market-driven efficiency of capitalist-oriented, free enterprise nations. But let's cite one example to see whether a disaster economy can teach us about fiscal policy.

Venezuela

We have already touched briefly on Venezuela. Venezuela used to be the richest nation in Latin America. That was in part due to the discovery of oil and in part because of reasonably good economic policy. In 1970, for instance, Venezuela ranked tenth for economic liberty according to Canada's Fraser Institute.[11] Today, however, Venezuela is suffering from economic crisis and ranks at the bottom of economic liberty. The hard left took power in the late 1990s and increased the size and scope of government. Since then, living standards have plummeted.

Is this because of fiscal policy? As illustrated by this chart from the Fraser Institute in Canada, there is little doubt that fiscal policy ("size of government") has moved in the wrong direction, evolving into autocratic dictatorship and many elements of a socialist economy. And since Venezuelan politicians also use

Size of Government Score by Year(s) - World Ranking Venezuela

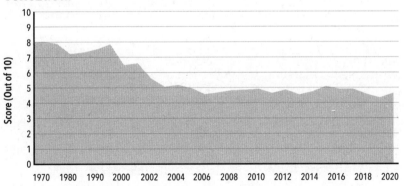

A bigger burden of government means a declining score. Venezuela's fiscal score is dropping because the burden of government has been increasing.

11 https://www.fraserinstitute.org/economic-freedom/dataset?geozone=world&-year=2021&page=dataset&min-year=2&max-year=0&filter=0.

inflationary monetary policy as a means of financing government spending, one can accurately argue that Venezuela's bad fiscal policy also causes bad scores for "sound money," leading to dramatic inflation.

But none of this means fiscal policy is the only cause of Venezuela's economic decline. Indeed, it does not even mean that fiscal policy is the leading cause. That's because Venezuela's scores have also plunged in areas that have nothing to do with fiscal policy, such as trade, regulation, the legal system, and property rights.

Conclusion

Other than disaster economies, which generally have terrible policy in many areas, the common theme to all these unfortunate examples is that governments get in trouble when budgets grow faster than the private sector. That means an ever-increasing fiscal burden. Governments then have no choice but to do a combination of three things: 1) borrow money to finance excessive spending, 2) raise taxes to finance excessive spending, and/or 3) print money to finance excessive spending.

All three options are harmful, though they do different types of damage. Financing big government with borrowing can lead to a debt crisis (like Greece). Financing big government with higher taxes can lead to economic stagnation (like many European nations). And financing big government by printing money can lead to inflation and economic instability (like Argentina).

In chapter 10, we will correlate good versus bad fiscal policy and the attendant good and bad results for a country.

CHAPTER 8

Prospering Countries

One way of choosing good policy is to look at which nations are successful and which ones are failures. It is smart to copy the prosperous ones! Especially if there is economic success for a long period.

But sometimes it is not easy to figure out why a country is prospering. There are lots of policy choices that determine whether a nation has a strong economy. Is the nation doing well because of low taxes and low spending? Or is it because there is no excessive regulation and red tape? Likewise, a country may have a weak economy because of high taxes and wasteful spending, but maybe the problem is inflation. Or harsh trade barriers. There can even be external factors that cause problems, such as sudden spikes in oil prices. Another challenge is that nations may have very good policy in some areas and very bad policy in other areas. So if the economy is just average, it becomes messy to figure out the impact of different policies.

There are organizations that measure economic policy in nations. The Fraser Institute publishes *Economic Freedom of the World*, for instance, and the Heritage Foundation publishes the *Index of Economic Freedom*. While the two publications are not identical, they both focus on:

- fiscal policy
- regulatory policy
- trade policy
- monetary policy
- government corruption
- property rights

This book focuses on fiscal policy, of course, and hopefully the information you read will give you insight into what policies work best and benefit all people in a given country. But it also is important to understand that good fiscal policy is just one piece of the puzzle.

With that important caveat, this chapter will look at real-world case studies that can teach us about good fiscal policy as evidenced by growth and economic prosperity. We will also examine whether certain states offer lessons about policies—which to follow and which to avoid.

If you want to know the main lessons without reading these real-world examples, here are the four top conditions for sensible fiscal policy:

1. Limit government spending so there is more room for the private sector to flourish.
2. Keep tax rates low so there are more incentives to work, save, invest, and be entrepreneurial.
3. Limit the growth of government spending.
4. Adhere to the idea that restraint is the only effective way to control deficits and debt.

Long-Run Success Stories

Let us start by looking at some nations that teach good lessons. Sadly, there are very few modern-day examples. At least with regard to governments that have managed to maintain good fiscal policy—or even decent fiscal policy—over a long period.

Switzerland

One of the world's most prosperous nations, Switzerland enjoys a relatively small burden of government spending when compared to other European countries. The most important measure of good fiscal policy is the size of government compared to the size of a nation's economy. In other words, is government a small burden on the private sector or a big burden?

This is why economists look at government spending as a share of gross domestic output (or GDP). As you can see from this table, Switzerland performs much better at this metric than its neighbors.

Pre- and Post-COVID, a Much Smaller Government Spending Burden in Switzerland

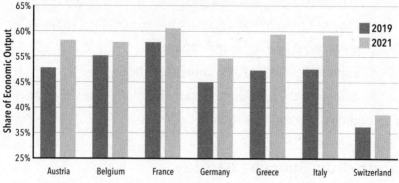

Why is Switzerland so much more fiscally responsible? There are two answers. First, the country has a federalist system, and most government activities are handled by the cantons (states) and municipalities. Unlike the United States, where the national government in Washington has expanded remarkably and added many new powers, the Swiss have done a very good job of protecting their decentralized system.

Federalism helps to restrain spending because regional governments (cantons or states) and local governments know that it is relatively simple for jobs and investment to escape if taxes get too high and there is too much waste. We see that in the United States, as people and businesses leave states such as New York and California and move to states such as Texas and Florida. The same thing happens in Switzerland. So the cantons compete with one another to have low taxes and responsible spending restraint.

The second reason for Switzerland's good performance is that voters approved a referendum in 2001 that imposes a spending cap on the central government. Technically known as the "debt brake," this measure was approved by an astounding 84.7 percent of voters. The debt brake limits spending growth to average revenue increases over a multiyear period, as calculated by the Swiss Federal Department of Finance. Some people think of the debt brake as being akin to a multiyear balanced budget requirement. There can be a deficit in one year (perhaps because of an economic downturn), but that deficit will be offset by mandated surpluses in other years.

Has Switzerland's spending cap been successful? The answer is clearly yes. Ever since the debt brake was adopted, government spending has increased by an average of just 2.2 percent per year. By contrast, overall government spending has increased by an average of 4.9 percent per year in the United States during the same period. And if you want to know why the Swiss spending cap is called a debt brake, this chart tells the answer.

Debts of the Confederation 1990–2017

Legend: Gross debt in CHF bn — Gross debt in % of GDP

By the way, politicians in Switzerland can increase the spending cap by raising taxes. But that is not easy since Swiss voters have a form of direct democracy. Tax rates can only be changed by a double-majority referendum, which means a majority of voters in a majority of cantons would have to agree. That does not happen very often. The Swiss people have the say on this, not the bureaucrats and politicians in government.

Hong Kong

We will start with a pessimistic observation that Hong Kong may have a grim future. When the British ceded the territory to China in 1997, the agreement was that Hong Kong would be a "special administrative region" with functional independence for another fifty years. China has not honored that agreement, asserting in 2014 that it has "comprehensive jurisdiction" over Hong Kong. And that was not an idle statement. A national security law was subsequently imposed that reduces Hong Kong's political freedoms.

The silver lining to that dark cloud is that Beijing has not substantively interfered with Hong Kong's economic policy. At least not yet. So let's look at fiscal policy in Hong Kong and contemplate the lessons that we can learn, even though there is not much optimism that China will allow those policies to remain much longer.

Hong Kong is most famous for having a very pro-growth system with low tax rates. It has a flat tax of 15 percent (known as the "standard rate"), but taxpayers may also choose to file using a progressive tax system if that means they pay less. Since the top rate in that system is only 17 percent, the overall tax burden on work and entrepreneurship is very low, regardless of which system gets used.

There also is a very low tax on income that is saved and invested. There is no capital gains tax and no death tax. There is also no double tax on interest income or dividend income. There are also very few loopholes, making the Hong Kong system very close to the pure system that has been championed by scholars such as Milton Friedman.

One big lesson from Hong Kong is that you need a small government if you want to keep taxes low in a fiscally responsible way. It is hard to predict what will happen in the future if China begins to interfere with Hong Kong's economic policy, but at least we can look at previous decades to learn some important lessons. As you can see from the chart, Hong Kong did a very good job of limiting the size of its government in the years when it was functionally independent. More specifically, the burden of spending,

Prior to Chinese Takeover, Government Spending Burden in Hong Kong only Half as Onerous as in the United States

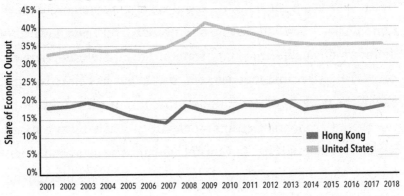

SOURCE: IMF

as a share of the economy, was far below the fiscal burden in the United States.

Why was Hong Kong successful? There are probably several factors, but its version of a constitution (the Basic Law) explicitly says, in Article 107, that government spending should not grow faster than the private sector.

> The Hong Kong Special Administrative Region shall follow the principle of keeping expenditure within the limits of revenues in drawing up its budget, and strive to achieve a fiscal balance, avoid deficits and keep the budget commensurate with the growth rate of its gross domestic product.

Because of sensible spending policy, Hong Kong naturally has not had a problem with deficits and debt. Indeed, it has almost no debt according to the International Monetary Fund.

Other Asian Tigers

Hong Kong is not the only successful small-government jurisdiction in Asia. A brief discussion of Singapore and Taiwan will also be informative. The small city-state of Singapore was relatively poor when it became independent in 1965 but has since become one of the world's richest nations. Since it routinely ranks in the top five for economic freedom, there are probably many reasons why it has grown so fast. Taiwan, meanwhile, also gets good scores for economic freedom. As with Singapore, there are presumably several policies that deserve credit.

Burden of Government Spending in Sigapore and Taiwan Is Less Than Half of the US Burden

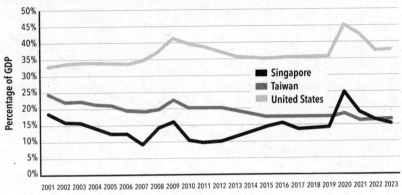

SOURCE: IMF

One common theme between the two jurisdictions is that they enjoy a relatively modest burden of government spending. Indeed, government spending as a share of economic output is less than half the US level. Equally impressive, there is a downward trend for spending, especially in Taiwan.

Having a small burden of government spending naturally means both Singapore and Taiwan have reasonably sensible tax policies—Singapore in particular, where the corporate rate is 17 percent and the personal income tax has a top tax rate of only 24 percent. Tax rates are higher in Taiwan than in Singapore, but still lower than the United States.

The very good policies in Singapore and the reasonably good policies in Taiwan have produced impressive results. The spending restraint has produced zero debt in Singapore and very low levels of debt in Taiwan, and both jurisdictions have enjoyed strong

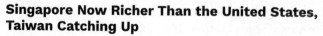

Singapore Now Richer Than the United States, Taiwan Catching Up

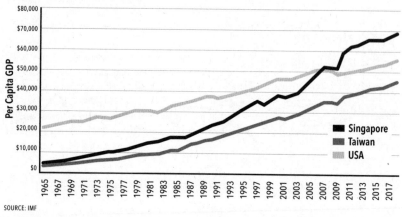

SOURCE: IMF

growth. As you can see from the chart, Singapore is now richer than the United States, based on per capita GDP. Per capita GDP in Taiwan has been growing nearly three times as fast as per capita GDP in the United States, so it is probably just a matter of time before Taiwan surpasses the US as well.

The common thread for Switzerland, Hong Kong, Singapore, and Taiwan is that government spending is constrained. This is the key point. When government takes less from the private sector, either by taxation or borrowing (or printing money), more is left in the productive sector to invest and grow.

Short-Run Success Stories

The ideal scenario is to have good long-run fiscal policy, which is why nations such as Switzerland and Singapore are good role models. But it also can be instructive to look at what happened when governments engaged in briefer periods of genuine spending restraint. Following, we will review some of the more prominent examples.

New Zealand

New Zealand's economy was stumbling in the 1980s. There was a range of bad policies, such as high tax rates, a heavy burden of government spending, protectionism, regulation, and subsidies.

Interestingly, it was a supposedly left-wing government that began moving the country in the right direction. After the Labour Party took power in the mid-1980s, it began to liberalize trade, lower tax rates, privatize, and deregulate.

But the big improvement in fiscal policy did not happen until the early 1990s. Building on the success of the Labour Party's reforms, the National Party decided it was time to control spending. Lawmakers were remarkably successful. As seen in the chart, there was a five-year spending freeze between 1992 and 1997.

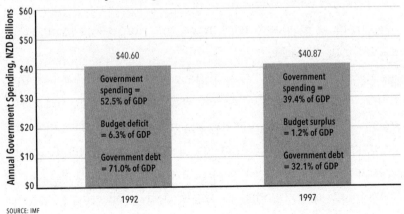

New Zealand Spending Freeze Produces Big Benefits

$40.60

Government spending = 52.5% of GDP

Budget deficit = 6.3% of GDP

Government debt = 71.0% of GDP

$40.87

Government spending = 39.4% of GDP

Budget surplus = 1.2% of GDP

Government debt = 32.1% of GDP

Annual Government Spending, NZD Billions

1992   1997

SOURCE: IMF

During this period, the economy grew, but spending did not. The burden of spending (measured as a share of GDP) fell dramatically.

But look also at what happened to deficits and debt. Because lawmakers dealt with the underlying problem of excessive spending, they automatically solved the symptom of red ink. New Zealand went from a big budget deficit to a budget surplus. The national debt, measured as a share of the economy, fell by more than half.

The period of spending restraint eventually came to an end, which is bad news. But the good news is that New Zealand lawmakers have largely preserved the progress that was achieved. The burden of government spending today is still about 40 percent of overall economic output.

Ireland

Forty years ago, Ireland was a very poor country by European standards. Now it is called the "Celtic Tiger" and is widely recognized as an economic success. The policy that gets the most attention is Ireland's 12.5 percent corporate tax rate. This pro-growth reform has attracted jobs and investment, thus improving living standards for Irish workers.

The low corporate rate is also a case study for what is sometimes referred to as supply-side economics. Back in the 1980s, Ireland's corporate tax rate was 50 percent and tax revenues were anemic, barely reaching 1 percent of economic output. Today, by contrast, corporate tax revenues average close to 3 percent of economic output. In other words, Ireland is collecting a lot more revenue at a much lower tax rate because its very competitive tax rate attracted significant industry.

But there is another good policy reform that gets very little attention. In the 1980s, back when Ireland was a poor nation, there was a very heavy burden of government spending. This fiscal burden was suffocating the economy and causing a buildup of debt. Irish lawmakers finally realized that something needed to change. They decided to restrain the growth of government. Indeed, they wound up freezing government spending between 1985 and 1989.

Ireland's Four-Year Spending Freeze Produces Big Benefits

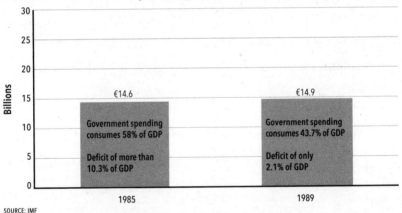

SOURCE: IMF

This gave the private sector some much-needed breathing room. Growth improved, and the burden of government spending fell as a share of GDP. And because there was progress tackling the problem of too much spending, the symptoms of deficits and debt became more manageable.

But we should not overstate Ireland's success. It has a low corporate tax rate, but other tax policies are very onerous. There was budgetary discipline in the late 1980s, but politicians since then have allowed far too much spending growth. And, yes, Ireland has very impressive economic numbers (such as per capita GDP), but that is partly a statistical quirk resulting from so many companies using Ireland as a base for their European operations.

Canada

Years of excessive spending under both Liberal and Conservative governments significantly increased Canada's fiscal burden. Chastened by fears of a fiscal crisis, politicians finally began to impose some fiscal discipline in 1992. Over the next five years, government spending, on average, grew less than 1 percent annually.

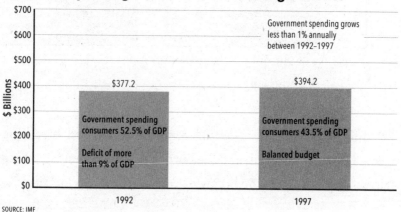

Canadian Spending Restraint Produces Big Benefits

SOURCE: IMF

This period of spending restraint paid big dividends. Because government grew slower than the economy, the overall burden of spending in Canada dropped by 9 percentage points of GDP—from 52.5 percent of economic output to 43.5 percent of output. This fiscal discipline also eliminated a large budget deficit. Red ink was equal to 9 percent of GDP in 1992. By 1997, Canada had a balanced budget.

The bad news is that Canada's period of spending restraint came to an end. But the good news is that there has not been any significant backsliding. Indeed, the overall spending burden today is slightly lower—as a share of GDP—than it was in 1997.

Baltic Spending Cuts

There was a global financial crisis in 2008. Politicians in most nations used the crisis as an excuse to enact wasteful spending packages. As you might expect, these "stimulus" schemes did not avert recessions. Instead, they exacerbated economic hardship by expanding national fiscal burdens.

But not all nations opted for more deficit spending. The Baltic nations of Estonia, Latvia, and Lithuania chose a different approach. They cut spending. Even more remarkably, they imposed genuine cuts, meaning spending actually went down (politicians in the United States, by contrast, claim they are cutting spending when the budget goes up, just not as fast as previously planned).

As illustrated in the following chart, Latvia led the way by cutting its budget by more than 13 percent between 2008 and

2010. Estonia also displayed fiscal rectitude, reducing the burden of spending by nearly 10 percent during that two-year period. And Lithuania deserves credit in for reducing outlays by 5 percent.

Baltic Nations Impose Genuine Spending Cuts in 2009 and 2010

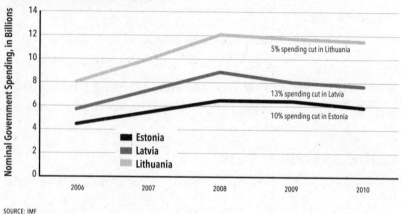

SOURCE: IMF

Sadly, the spending cuts only lasted a couple of years, but two years of genuine spending cuts is better than big spending increases—which is what happened in many other nations when the financial crisis hit.

Moreover, the Baltic nations have focused on implementing tax systems that don't penalize success with high tax rates. This helps to explain why they are the more prosperous nations that emerged from the collapse of the Soviet Union.

Sweden

Some people think of Sweden as having a socialist economy. This is not accurate; it has a free enterprise/market economy. It has high tax rates and a big welfare state, of course, but it does not have the policies—government-owned factories, central planning, and price controls—that you find in genuinely socialist economies.

That being said, the Scandinavian country can teach us a very important lesson about how to reverse a fiscal disaster. Decades of extraordinary spending growth (government spending increasing at double-digit rates between 1980 and 1992) and lax monetary policy combined to push Sweden into a deep three-year recession in the early 1990s.

Lawmakers recognized that policy had to change to restore financial and fiscal stability. Starting in 1993, the Swedish government was put on a diet. Over a nine-year period, the burden of government spending grew by an average of just 1.9 percent

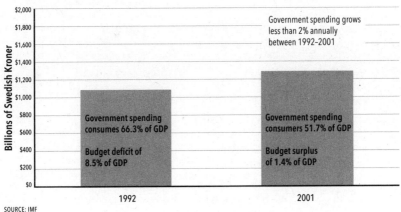

Swedish Spending Restraint Produces Big Benefits

Billions of Swedish Kroner

Government spending grows less than 2% annually between 1992-2001

1992: Government spending consumes 66.3% of GDP; Budget deficit of 8.5% of GDP

2001: Government spending consumers 51.7% of GDP; Budget surplus of 1.4% of GDP

SOURCE: IMF

117

annually. That was meaningful spending restraint, especially since inflation averaged over 2 percent during those years.

This dramatic shift generated big benefits. As shown in the chart, the burden of government spending fell from 66 percent of economic output to less than 52 percent of economic output. And for those who care about government deficits, there was a similarly dramatic shift. A large budget deficit of 8.5 percent of GDP in 1992 became a budget surplus of 1.4 percent nine years later.

The period of spending restraint did end, which is bad news. But the good news is that Sweden (like New Zealand and Canada) has not moved back in the wrong direction. Indeed, there's been a small amount of additional progress over the past twenty years. The burden of spending is now less than 50 percent of GDP in Sweden.

CHAPTER 9

Fiscal Lessons from the United States

There are good and bad lessons to be learned from fiscal policy in the United States. It all depends on the years being examined. One important thing to understand is that there was not any fiscal policy for much of America's history. Yes, the federal government spent money and imposed taxes, but the fiscal burden of government was trivially small for the nation's first 150 years.

The words *trivially small* are not an exaggeration. Up until the 1930s, with the exceptions of the Civil War and World War I, total federal spending consumed less than 3 percent of the economy's output (gross domestic product, or GDP). To put that number in context, the burden of federal spending in 2023 is estimated to consume more than 24 percent of GDP, at least eight times bigger as a share of the economy.

For readers who like wading into the details, here's a table from a report titled "An Economic History of Federal Spending and Debt," published in 2015 by the Joint Economic Committee.[12] As you can see, federal spending, federal revenue, and federal debt were negligible burdens prior to the 1930s. For most of those years, the federal government had budget surpluses.

POPULATION, GDP, AND FEDERAL REVENUE, SPENDING & DEBT AVERAGES BY DECADE								
Decade	Population Growth	Real Estimated GDP & GDP Growth Annual Average Growth Rate	Total Revenue Annual Average as a % of Est. GDP / GDP	Total Spending Annual Average as a % of Est. GDP / GDP	Non-Interest Spending Average as a % of Est. GDP / GDP	Public Debt Average as a % of Est. GDP / GDP	Years of Surplus	Years of Deficit
1790s	34.82%	6.31%	1.90%	1.95%	1.01%	24.33%	6	4
1800s	32.28%	3.71%	2.32%	1.59%	0.93%	13.07%	9	1
1810s	29.34%	3.11%	2.63%	2.85%	2.24%	10.78%	5	5
1820s	30.33%	4.41%	2.57%	1.93%	1.44%	9.40%	8	2
1830s	28.94%	3.59%	2.27%	1.76%	1.73%	0.80%	7	3
1840s	32.07%	4.95%	1.44%	1.68%	1.60%	1.46%	4	5
1850s	30.79%	5.39%	1.66%	1.63%	1.55%	1.43%	7	3
1860s	23.87%	3.13%	3.62%	6.64%	5.63%	22.98%	5	5
1870s	22.56%	5.28%	3.67%	3.19%	1.94%	25.57%	10	0
1880s	22.52%	5.21%	2.94%	2.12%	1.69%	12.55%	10	0
1890s	18.10%	3.27%	2.36%	2.46%	2.22%	6.91%	4	6
1900s	19.11%	2.49%	2.12%	2.08%	1.99%	4.18%	5	5
1910s	13.42%	2.72%	3.30%	6.46%	6.19%	10.40%	4	6
1920s	13.50%	3.14%	4.56%	3.67%	2.70%	22.65%	10	0
1930s	6.52%	2.12%	5.19%	8.47%	8.73%	38.41%	0	10
1940s	14.14%	5.96%	14.82%	24.08%	22.75%	78.41%	3	7
1950s	16.65%	3.91%	17.08%	17.35%	16.10%	53.35%	4	6
1960s	11.63%	4.40%	17.35%	18.15%	16.91%	35.48%	1	9
1970s	9.42%	3.21%	17.37%	19.61%	18.13%	25.66%	0	10
1980s	8.72%	3.24%	17.65%	21.59%	18.78%	35.14%	0	10
1990s	111.90%	3.34%	18.17%	19.65%	16.82%	43.80%	3	7
2000s	8.70%	1.73%	16.57%	19.97%	18.44%	39.26%	1	9
2010s	2.24%	1.95%	16.17%	21.71%	20.33%	70.81%	0	4

12 http://www.jec.senate.gov/public/_cache/files/c90da849-986a-41d3-ab20-77f38a393d85/20150910-jec-spendingstudy.pdf.

During those years, the federal government did very little other than maintain a military. There was no Department of Health and Human Services, no Department of Transportation, no Department of Education, no Department of Energy, and no welfare programs. The only entitlement program was benefits for veterans.

One advantage of very small government was that there was no income tax for much of American history. Nor were there payroll taxes, corporate taxes, death taxes, or capital gains taxes. The federal government was funded by trade taxes and a handful of excise taxes. And even when an income tax was imposed in 1913, politicians claimed it was for the purpose of enabling lower trade taxes, not to finance bigger government.

Unfortunately, giving Washington politicians the power to tax income subsequently enabled a massive expansion in the size and scope of the federal government. That's the bad news. The good news (from an analytical perspective) is that events of the past hundred-plus years have given us all sorts of evidence about the types of tax and spending policies that work . . . and the ones that don't. In what follows, we will examine periods of major change in fiscal policy and the lessons that can be learned from them.

The 1920s

As outlined previously, the federal government in the 1920s was much smaller than it is today. But two things happened that decade that deserve attention. Indeed, these two things teach us lessons that still apply to fiscal policy in the twenty-first century.

The first big event of the 1920s is that lawmakers in Washington cut spending. And unlike today, when the definition has been watered down (a smaller-than-desired increase is considered a budget cut), overall government spending was truly reduced, and by significant amounts. Here's a chart showing what happened to federal spending between 1920 and 1924. Remarkably, overall government spending was reduced by more than 50 percent. The budget shrank from more than $6 billion in 1920 to less than $3 billion in 1924.

President Harding Reduced the Burden of Government Spending

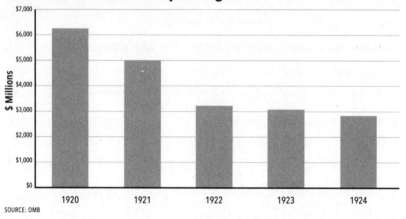

SOURCE: OMB

But the lesson is not simply that it is possible to cut spending. What is also noteworthy is that the economy was in a deep economic downturn in 1920 and the spending cuts helped enable a rapid economic recovery. This approach is considered economic heresy by modern-day "Keynesians," who argue that government should spend more money to help a weak economy. The 1920s, though, are a real-world example of helping the economy by shrinking the burden of government spending.

The 1920s also teach an important lesson about tax policy. At the start of the decade, the top tax rate was 73 percent, a legacy of the huge tax rate increases during World War I. Lawmakers in Washington realized these confiscatory tax rates punished people for working, saving, and investing. They realized punitive tax policy discouraged entrepreneurship. So they slashed tax rates, especially the onerous tax rates that applied to upper-income households. As shown in the chart, the top tax rate initially fell to 58 percent and then was dramatically lowered to 25 percent in the middle of the decade.

Lower Tax Rates in the 1920s Meant More Tax Revenue

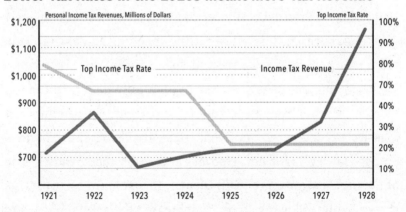

SOURCES: Tax Foundation; "The Mellon and Kennedy Tax Cuts: A Review and Analysis," Staff Study Joint Economic Comittee, June 18, 1982.

But notice what happened to tax revenue. After a blip in the early part of the decade, revenue rose. And revenues increased most rapidly after the top tax rate fell to 25 percent. Moreover, most of the increased revenue came from the rich. Indeed, the share of income tax revenue paid by the rich jumped from less than 50 percent to nearly 80 percent.

In other words, the 1920s showed that there is indeed a Laffer Curve: tax rates can be so high that the government actually loses revenue. Indeed, the treasury secretary at the time, Andrew Mellon, famously remarked that, "The history of taxation shows that taxes which are inherently excessive are not paid. The high rates inevitably put pressure upon the taxpayer to withdraw his capital from productive business."[13]

The 1930s

Just like the 1920s, the 1930s began with a deep economic downturn. But that's the only thing the two decades have in common. That's because Presidents Hoover and Roosevelt chose a completely different approach. Instead of cutting spending and lowering tax rates, they both followed a tax-and-spend approach.

Regarding tax policy, Hoover dramatically increased the top income tax rate, from 25 percent to 63 percent. He also imposed massive tax increases on global trade, thanks to the infamous Smoot-Hawley Tariff Act. Hoover's record on the spending side of the fiscal ledger was equally dismal. In just four short years, as shown by the following chart, he increased the annual burden of federal spending by 47 percent. But this was a period of falling prices. If the budget numbers are adjusted for inflation, Hoover was even more of a big spender.

13 Andrew Mellon, *Taxation: The People's Business* (New York: Macmillan, 1924).

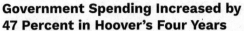

**Government Spending Increased by
47 Percent in Hoover's Four Years**

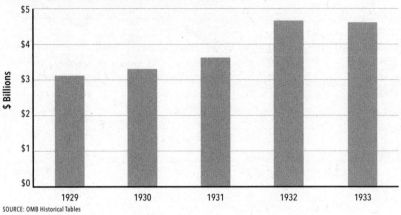

SOURCE: OMB Historical Tables

Hoover was punished for his bad performance, losing in a landslide in the 1932 election. Unfortunately, Franklin Roosevelt basically continued Hoover's policies. He increased the top tax rate to 77 percent, and then to 79 percent. That was misguided, of course, but his biggest mistake was probably his decision to continue Hoover's approach to spending. Over the next eight years, as shown by this additional chart, the burden of government spending doubled.

There are two big lessons we can learn from the Hoover–Roosevelt years. The first lesson is that the Hoover–Roosevelt tax increases (including both trade taxes and income taxes) were not successful. Alan Reynolds of the Cato Institute shared the most compelling evidence. Looking through IRS data, he found that upper-income taxpayers reported more than $6 billion of annual income to the IRS in the late 1920s. In the 1930s, after Hoover and

Federal Budget Doubles in FDR's First Two Terms

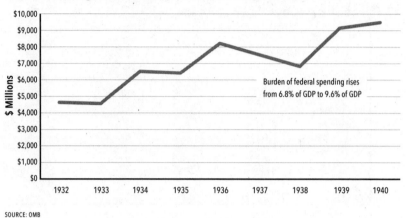

Burden of federal spending rises
from 6.8% of GDP to 9.6% of GDP

SOURCE: OMB

Roosevelt raised tax rates, the amount of taxable income reported by that same group of taxpayers never rose above $2 billion.

The second lesson is that the high-tax, high-spend approach was bad news for the economy. Instead of a quick and strong recovery, like the United States enjoyed in the 1920s when taxes and spending were going down, the economy was very anemic in the 1930s.

There were many reasons why the economy was weak for the entire decade, so it would be inappropriate to assert that the Hoover–Roosevelt fiscal policies deserve all the blame. But surely the heavier fiscal burden is partly responsible. That's because the higher tax rates discouraged people from engaging in productive behavior. And the increasing burden of government spending diverted resources from the productive sector of the economy.

Ironically, some people look at the 1930s and think that the Hoover–Roosevelt policies were successful. They think that the excessive spending of the 1930s was a victory for Keynesian economics, even though the economy did not recover until World War II. This is a bizarre misinterpretation of history. The economy recovered in the 1920s when taxes and spending were reduced, and the economy languished in the 1930s when taxes and spending were increased.

You have heard the terms the Roaring Twenties and the Great Depression. This is an explanation of how government policies, and in particular fiscal policies, fostered growth in the '20s and economic malaise in the '30s.[14]

Let's close with a quote that perfectly summarizes the failure of fiscal policy in the 1930s. Henry Morgenthau, President Roosevelt's treasury secretary, admitted to the House Ways and Means Committee in April 1939: "Now, gentlemen, we have tried spending money. We are spending more than we have ever spent before and it does not work . . . I say after eight years of this administration we have just as much unemployment as when we started . . . and an enormous debt, to boot."

The 1960s

A few notable things happened in the 1960s. With regards to government spending, 1965 was a very unfortunate year. President Lyndon Johnson and the Democratic Congress enacted two

---

14 There was, of course, a stock market crash in 1929. Some researchers have cited the role of protectionism since the crash occurred as politicians were pushing the Smoot-Hawley Tariff Act. That obviously had a depressing effect on investor confidence, so it is a partial explanation. The bigger problem, however, was that there were major financial imbalances because of the clumsy way governments sought to reestablish the gold standard after World War I—all of which was exacerbated by the terms of the Treaty of Versailles.

entitlement programs—Medicare and Medicaid—that would become major long-run problems for the United States (by way of reminder, Medicare is the government's health program for the elderly, and Medicaid is the government's health program for the poor).

How much of a long-run problem? Charles Blahous of the Mercatus Center (former trustee for the Social Security and Medicare programs) performed a comprehensive study to determine which politicians caused America's fiscal imbalance.[15] Table 2 from his study finds that Johnson single-handedly did more damage than any other politician (or group of politicians). Notice, also, that House and Senate Democrats from the same era were the second and fourth worst in terms of long-run fiscal consequences. And if you read his report, the overwhelming reason for the bad scores is that Medicare and Medicaid have created huge long-run fiscal problems for the nation.

There was, however, some good fiscal news in the 1960s. President Kennedy proposed across-the-board tax rate reductions in 1963. He was assassinated in November of that year, but Congress approved his tax plan in 1964. The legislation included a slight reduction in the federal corporate tax rate (from 52 percent to 48 percent), but the highlight of the legislation was a significant reduction in tax rates on personal income. The top tax rate dropped from 91 percent to 70 percent, and other tax rates were reduced as well.

---

15 https://papers.ssrn.com/sol3/papers.cfm?abstract_id=3967577.

Shares of Responsibility for Long-term Federal Fiscal Imbalance

Contributor	Share of responsibility for long-term fiscal imbalance (%)
Johnson (Lyndon B.)	14.8
US House Democrats, 1965–1972	14.7
Nixon (Richard M.)	14.6
US Senate Democrats, 1965–1972	11.8
Obama (Barack H.)	10.9
Bush (George W.)	4.1
Trump (Donald J.)	3.8
US House Democrats, 2007–2010	3.2
US Senate Republicans, 1965–1972	2.9
US Senate Democrats, 2007–2010	2.5
US House Republicans, 2003–2006	2.0
US House Democrats, 2019–2020	1.9
US Senate Republicans, 2003–2006	1.6
US House Republicans, 2011–2014	1.5
US Senate Republicans, 2019–2020	1.5
US Senate Democrats, 2011–2014	1.2
Bush (George H. W.)	1.1
US House Democrats, 1987–1994	0.9
US House Republicans, 2015–2018	0.8
US Senate Democrats, 1987–1994	0.7
US Senate Republicans, 2007–2010	0.6
Reagan (Ronald W.)	0.6
US Senate Republicans, 2015–2018	0.6
US Senate Democrats, 2003–2006	0.4
US Senate Democrats, 2019–2020	0.4
US Senate Republicans, 2011–2014	0.3
US Senate Republicans, 1987–1994	0.2
US Senate Democrats, 2015–2018	0.2

Note: House = House of Representatives
a. Sum of percentages is less than 100 owing to rounding. Underlying numbers, when calculated to more significant figures, add up to 100.0
Source: Author's calculations based on data from the Congressional Budget Office

What was the impact of the Kennedy tax cuts? The most notable consequence is not that revenues increased, but rather that upper-income taxpayers had a Laffer Curve response. As shown in the chart, taxpayers in the higher tax brackets substantially increased both their taxable income and their tax payments in response to lower tax rates.

Rich Pay More Under Kennedy Tax Cuts

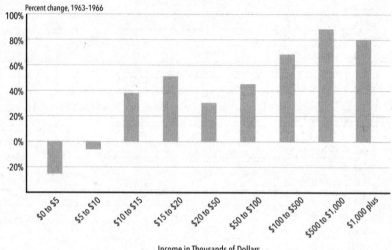

SOURCE: "The Mellon and Kennedy Tax Cuts: A Review and Analysis," Study, Joint Economic Committee, June 18, 1982.

Here's a very relevant statement from President John F. Kennedy. Speaking to the Economic Club of New York in 1962, he observed that, "An economy hampered by restrictive tax rates will never produce enough revenues to balance our budget just as it will never produce enough jobs or enough profits. . . . it is a paradoxical truth that tax rates are too high today and tax revenues are too low and the soundest way to raise the revenues in the long run is to cut the rates now."

The 1980s

The economy was a mess when Ronald Reagan took office. High inflation was wreaking havoc with the economy, with prices increasing at double-digit rates and interest rates climbing to record levels. That inflation also produced bracket creep, which is when rising incomes push people into higher tax brackets, even though their inflation-adjusted pay has not increased. It's a stealth tax increase. As explained by the San Francisco Federal Reserve Bank in a 1982 article, "the combination of sustained inflation and a progressive tax structure can result in a sharp increase in tax liabilities without legislative action."[16]

That is the bad news. The good news is that bracket creep created enormous pressure for tax reform. And that's what Ronald Reagan delivered. Like President Kennedy, he delivered across-the-board rate reductions as part of his 1981 Economic Recovery Tax Act. That law brought the top tax rate down from 70 percent to 50 percent and reduced other tax rates as well. That legislation was then followed by the Tax Reform Act of 1986, which further lowered the top tax rate down to 28 percent.

What lessons can we learn from Reagan's tax policies? The obvious lesson is that better tax policy helped produce an economic renaissance for the country. But there were many policies during the Reagan years that led to more prosperity. So rather than getting bogged down in a discussion of which reforms deserves the most credit for the Reagan boom, let's focus on the more narrow issue of what fiscal experts sometimes refer to as

16 https://www.frbsf.org/economic-research/files/el82-18.pdf.

"revenue feedback." In plain English, let us look at what the Reagan tax cuts can teach us about the Laffer Curve and class warfare.

Critics complain that Reagan was being unfair to lower the top tax rate. They said rich people would not pay enough and that the government would lose too much revenue. Fortunately, there is an easy way to determine whether these complaints are accurate. The IRS periodically publishes The Statistics of Income, which provides considerable detail for different segments of the population about how much income they earned and how much tax they paid.

1980 Taxes Paid on Income Over $200,000

	1980 Returns	1980 Taxable Income	1980 Income Tax Paid
$200,00-$500,000	99,971	$22,696,007	$11,089,114
$500,000-$1,000,000	12,397	$6,512,424	$3,613,195
$1,000,000+	4,389	$7,013,225	$4,301,111
Total	116,757	$36,221,656	$19,003,420

1988 Taxes Paid on Income Over $200,000

	1988 Returns	1988 Taxable Income	1988 Income Tax Paid
$200,00-$500,000	547,239	$134,655,949	$38,446,620
$500,000-$1,000,000	114,652	$67,552,225	$19,040,602
$1,000,000+	61,896	$150,744,777	$42,254,821
Total	723,697	$352,952,951	$99,742,043

Source: Internal Revenue Service

More than six times as many rich people	Nearly ten times as much taxable income	More than five times as much tax revenue

So what happens if we compare the data for 1980, when the top tax rate was 70 percent, and the data for 1988, when the top tax rate had dropped to 28 percent? As you can see from the preceding table, taxpayers making more than $200,000 per year paid five times more tax in 1988 and they did in 1980. This was not just the Laffer Curve. It was the Laffer Curve on steroids.

There are caveats, of course, which should make us cautious about exaggerating the impact of lower tax rates. There was some population growth during those years, and also inflation, so there almost surely would have been some increase in the number of returns from rich taxpayers, as well as some increase in taxable income. But it also seems clear that the dramatic reduction in tax rates encouraged more people to earn more income, and this meant that the IRS actually collected more revenue from rich people.

There are also lessons from the spending side of the fiscal equation during the Reagan years. Most notably, Reagan showed that it is possible to constrain, and even reduce, the welfare state. Between 1981 and 1989, the overall burden of government spending dropped from 21.6 percent of GDP to 20.6 percent of GDP. That is somewhat impressive considering that government has a tendency to become bigger over time.[17]

But it does not capture what Reagan achieved. If you remove defense spending (necessary to counter the Soviet Union) and net interest spending (the one category that is genuinely untouchable),

17 The national debt increased during the Reagan years, rising from 25.5 percent of GDP at the end of 1980 to 39.9 percent of GDP at the end of 1988. Almost all of the increase occurred as a result of the 1981–82 recession, before Reagan's policies took effect.

what's left is overall domestic spending—both discretionary and mandatory. Remarkably, Reagan was able to reduce the burden of domestic spending by 2.5 percentage points of GDP, more than three times as much as the next most frugal president.

Change in Burden of Domestic Spending

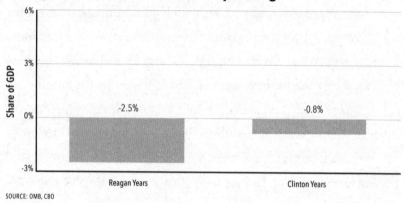

SOURCE: OMB, CBO

Sadly, Reagan's legacy was undermined by his successor. In 1990, President George H. W. Bush agreed to a fiscal plan that raised taxes and raised spending. The net result is that red ink, which was declining as Reagan left office, suddenly spiked upward.

Other Notable Fiscal Events

This look at the 1920s, 1930s, 1960s, and 1980s covers some highlights (or lowlights) of America's fiscal history. But this does not mean that nothing interesting happened in other decades.

- **The 1940s:** During the first part of the decade, the focus was on winning World War II. In the latter half of the decade, supporters of Keynesian economics looked foolish because they predicted a return to depression when demobilization from the war resulted in huge reductions in government spending. What actually happened? In just two years, the burden of federal spending dropped from more than 40 percent of GDP down to about 15 percent of GDP. But there was no return to depression, just a short downturn as the economy adjusted to millions of returning troops.

- **The 1950s:** Other than a temporary surge in defense spending because of the Korean War, there were very few fiscal changes during this decade. The most interesting factoid is that confiscatory 90 percent-plus tax rates (a legacy of World War II) so discouraged people from being highly productive that only eight people had earned enough income to be in that tax bracket at the end of the decade.

- **The 1970s:** As noted, this decade was most notable for President Nixon's reckless spending during the early part of the decade and the inflation-induced bracket creep throughout the decade that resulted in massive unlegislated tax increases on American households.

- **The 1990s:** The most remarkable thing about this decade was that the combination of a Democratic president and a Republican Congress produced genuine spending restraint, which resulted in budget surpluses between 1998–2000.

- **The 2000s:** President George W. Bush was a big spender and President Barack Obama was a big spender, with the worst policies happening in Bush's last year (the TARP bailout) and Obama's first year (the failed stimulus).

- **The 2010s:** The most notable fiscal event this decade is that "Tea Party" Republicans took control of Congress and significantly slowed the growth of spending. Indeed, the nation enjoyed a de facto five-year spending freeze early in the decade, which significantly reduced the burden of spending and therefore reduced red ink.

The Spending Binge Has Ended

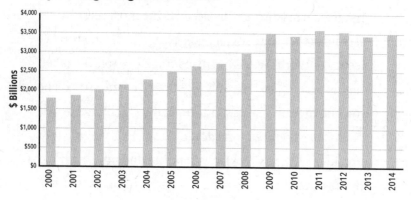

SOURCE: OMB, CBO

- **The 2020s:** This decade has barely begun, but the most noteworthy event is that President Biden has continued President Trump's policy of more and more spending.

The bottom line is that America's modern fiscal history confirms that spending restraint and low tax rates are the formula for economic prosperity and fiscal prudence.

CHAPTER 10

Lessons from the Real World

In section II, we examined the good, the bad, and the ugly from various economies as well as the good and bad from the history of the United States. There are clear teaching moments to be found as we examine what was done and the results. The whole purpose of this section is to make it clear that good policy works and bad policy does not. To bring this home, we can learn much from our examination of the real world.

Once we understand the lessons, we can apply them to this country to emulate success and avoid failure. Let's review the major lessons learned so far.

Successes

When we examine Switzerland, Hong Kong, Taiwan, and Singapore, there are obvious common threads. They have governments that are limited in size; they are fiscally responsible; they have lower taxation because the cost of government is relatively low; and they have modest indebtedness in relation to the size of the economy.

Perhaps most importantly, government spending very rarely grows faster than the private sector. And when government spending is controlled, there is very little temptation to raise taxes, issue debt, or print money. This leads to faster growth in the economy and a rising standard of living as measured by GDP per capita. They do not all have the same standard of living because the policies are not identical, and some have had good policy for a longer period.

They all rate high on the scale of economic freedom. That means the individuals are not controlled as much by government regulation, and there is good rule of law in place to protect property rights.

It is critical that we understand why these policies are effective, and economic theory explains this well.

Failures

When we examine some of the major problems countries experience, we see common threads that led to their plights—governments that grew faster than the economy for an extended period and had major deficits over the long term; governments that were large in relation to the economy, taking high taxes or borrowing significantly from the private sector; and governments that did not have sound economic policies and scored lower on the Index of Economic Freedom.

Some of these have failed and had to be "bailed out" by international organizations. They all had low growth rates, as their policies did not promote growth and a rising standard of living.

Others had socialist or autocratic governments, causing the economies to fail completely on economic freedom. They were unable to produce enough even to cover the necessities of the general population. Some of these improved as they liberalized their economies and incorporated basic market economic principals such as private property and rule of law, protecting individual property, and providing incentives to individuals to develop businesses and grow.

United States History

When we look at the history of the US, it is clear that the same principles apply. The country grew and prospered when the government was smaller and was fiscally responsible. But when the government grew faster than the private sector, and deficits became commonplace and grew dramatically, problems appeared. As discussed in section I, this process has accelerated since 2001. Now the United States is on the verge of serious fiscal problems. The debts of this country exceed the size of the economy, approaching 130 percent with much more projected. If we continue on the current course, we will be the next Greece or Venezuela.

Reviewing the Major Principles

LIMITED GOVERNMENT: Government is funded in one of three ways:

1. taxation
2. borrowing from the public
3. printing money

By having smaller government expenditures, less is taken from the public by way of taxes and borrowing. That leaves more capital in the hands of the public, the only productive sector in an economy; that capital will be invested in producing more goods and services. That is growth: the more goods and services that are produced and the faster they grow, the faster the economy grows.

Printing money, as we have learned, works just like economic theory says it will. If you print money faster than output grows, this will cause inflation. It is a simple concept of supply and demand. Extra money chasing fewer goods will bid prices up.

FISCAL RESPONSIBILITY: Governments can manage their fiscal affairs in many ways. They can live within their means, meaning limits on the growth of government spending, which is an effective receipt for a balanced budget or a surplus. Alternatively, they can spend more than they take in in taxes, creating budget deficits that have to be financed somehow—borrowing or printing money, as noted.

Borrowing to a limited degree from time to time may not be seriously harmful. But as we have seen, continuously borrowing or printing excessively will lead to a crisis. The debts will become unmanageable and ultimately (when the investors lose confidence in a country's ability to pay) the country becomes insolvent and cannot operate on its own. This has happened to many countries over the years, and all had to be bailed out by international funds.

ECONOMIC FREEDOM: Overbearing governments stifle the incentives and productivity of an economy. It is clear those countries that do best have the highest scores on this index. Sound trade policy, sound fiscal policy, sound regulatory policy—these are all part of the index. When good policy is prevalent in all these areas, good things happen for the economy and the well-being of the citizens of that country.

What the Hell Can We Do about It?

Overview

In section I, we discussed the dire situation we face in the United States. We are bankrupt, and the future looks even worse. The Department of the Treasury says it clearly: "The current fiscal path is unsustainable."

In section II, we reviewed various examples of fiscal and spending policy at home and abroad. This left no doubt about how different policies get different results, what works and what doesn't for improving the lives of the citizens of any organized political entity.

Now, in section III, we explore ideas for restoring fiscal sanity. It is not a detailed proposal of exactly what must be done—that is beyond the scope of this book. The specific details must come from a panel or commission of experts from many different fields, appointed by our representatives and accountable to them. In the Introduction, we explained that the US Ship of State was on course to collide with the proverbial iceberg someday. That outcome is not inevitable. We can change course and fix our problems—but if we do not fix them, we will see the greatest Ponzi scheme on Earth fail. We must not let that happen, for our benefit as well as those of our kids, grand-kids, and all future generations to come.

In section III, we cover many of the most important issues, but by no means all of them. Remember, this book is for you, the voting public, the folks on Main Street. The solutions to our problems must be acted upon by our representatives, and an action plan must be put in place. The politicians will act if there is public support; without it, nothing will be done. We must communicate with our representatives so that they will get the message and act. If they don't act responsibly, then we must vote for someone who will get the job done.

In chapter 5, "Entitlements," we explained what the most important entitlements are and described the key problems each program faces. These programs add over $1 trillion to our deficit annually and will get much worse over time. In section III, we dig deeper into the specifics of each and give a general discussion of what is needed to get them back on track.

Chapter 11: Fixing Social Security

As we learned in section I, the demographics of the Social Security system have changed its economic viability. It cannot work as now structured and will exhaust its funding in 2033, based on the most recent projections. When that occurs, the current law requires benefits to be cut to match revenue. This would be catastrophic for the families and individuals who depend on it. We must fix the problem by law to avoid this. In this chapter, we outline some ideas that will bring Social Security into long-range sustainability.

Chapter 12: Fixing Medicare

As you have learned, there are three major parts of Medicare: Part A for hospitalization, Part B for medical, and Part D for drugs. These impose an enormous burden on the national budget and must be addressed if we are to get to fiscal sanity. In this chapter, we outline ideas to bring down the deficits in these programs.

Chapter 13: Fixing Medicaid

This program, and related programs, help low-income Americans get medical care. The cost of this program is shared between the federal government and the states. Approximately two-thirds of the cost is paid by the federal government to the states, which administer the program. The cost has risen to over

$500 billion per year. Chapter 13 explores ways to curtail Medicaid's growth to minimize the cost to the federal government.

Chapter 14: Tax Policy

The current IRS code is 75,000 pages and unintelligible to any mortal. Over the years it has been used to promote special interests of all kinds. It has become so full of loopholes, incentives, and subsidies that the effective tax rates are hard to determine. It is very progressive, with disproportionate taxes falling on the wealthy, yet many still say "tax the rich." That is already happening, but even if we taxed all the income of this group, it would not pay for all our government's expenses and proposed programs. There are a number of policy changes that could be made to streamline the code and make this a more balanced and fair system.

Chapter 15: Federalism

The Constitution of the United States spells out the tasks of the federal government. We have gone far away from that model into tasks the federal government doesn't need to do. Some activities do not need to be done by anyone; others are best done by the states or individuals. In this chapter, we look at some ways to streamline the federal government.

There is much to be done and little time to do it. Changing the course that the Ship of State is on will be very time consuming and slow, but it must be done before we crash and burn. Section III is merely a broad review of the major issues. The federal government needs to appoint a group of professionals and charge them with examining the real issues and developing solutions. Then they must implement them, before it is too late.

CHAPTER 11

Fixing Social Security

Overview

In chapter 5 we reviewed entitlements with an emphasis on Social Security, Medicare, and Medicaid. In this chapter we will focus on the specific problems of Social Security, its future, and how we can address the problems without harming anyone who is currently getting benefits or will get them in the future. Given the broken nature of the current system, it won't be easy, but it must be done.

Is the Social Security system a Ponzi scheme within a Ponzi scheme? We are paying in, and the current beneficiaries are taking it out. This type of pay-as-you-go system works so long as there are ever-larger numbers of younger workers. But that is no longer the case. There will not be enough money when today's workers become would-be beneficiaries. We can only be paid benefits from the contributions of those who are still paying into the system. That is how all Ponzi schemes end.

Some politicians shout that we cannot touch Social Security. Nonsense. It must be fixed; it is badly broken and will fail if we do nothing.

Social Security is a pay-as-you-go system. That means the income from employees and employers today is used to pay benefits for those who are retired. There is no account in your name, and promised benefits are not guaranteed.

There is a Social Security Trust Fund, but it is solely for bookkeeping purposes. It does not hold real assets. In the past, when Social Security taxes were higher than benefit payments, the federal government spent the money on other programs and gave the trust fund a special type of IOU from the Treasury Department.

Now that benefit payments are higher than taxes, the IOUs in the trust fund are being redeemed in order to ensure recipients get all the benefits they have been promised. But the Treasury Department redeems the special IOUs by simply borrowing more money. As Bill Clinton's Office of Management and Budget explained back in 1999:

These balances are available to finance future benefit payments and other trust fund expenditures—but only in a bookkeeping sense. . . . They do not consist of real economic assets that can be drawn down in the future to fund benefits. Instead, they are claims on the Treasury, that, when redeemed, will have to be financed by raising taxes, borrowing from the public, or reducing benefits or other expenditures.[18]

But there is one way in which the trust fund is real. At the point when there are no longer IOUs in the trust fund, the law requires that benefits be cut to match the level of tax payments. This would require an estimated 24 percent decrease in benefits initially, rising over time to 26 percent as the deficits continue to increase.

Politicians could change the law so that full benefits are still paid. But since the program's inflation-adjusted cash flow deficit is more than $60 trillion over the next seventy-five years, that would be an expensive option. This unfunded liability would have to be covered by some adjustments to the system or by general revenues from the government.

It's a Ponzi Scheme

Social Security is another Ponzi scheme with no end in sight under current law. It either must be force balanced, as currently required by cutting benefits; be supplemented from general revenues to maintain benefits (requiring a change in the law), which would make future federal government deficits significantly worse; or be reformed in some manner. It is unlikely that politicians would cut benefits to retirees, which would be unfair and particularly devastating to lower-income seniors who depend on this income. Knowing that the

---

18 See page 337 of http://www.gpo.gov/fdsys/pkg/BUDGET-2000-PER/pdf/BUDGET-2000-PER.pdf.

current projected federal deficits are already unsustainable, maintaining the benefits for Social Security from general government revenues would make a bad problem worse. Accordingly, there is an absolute need for the system to be reformed.

Conventional Approaches to Reform

There are a number of things that can be done to try to fix the current pay-as-you-go system and could balance the future shortfall in the short run. These are very expensive Band-Aids to a broken system, and they will require heavy taxation on middle- and lower-income Americans, as well as upper-income citizens, to meet the needs. It would be impossible to tweak the system enough to achieve balance in the future without raising taxes significantly on everyone. And this fix might not work for the long term. The longer we wait, the more difficult the solution becomes, as the whole system moves closer to insolvency.

Here are some of the conventional approaches. This is not an exhaustive list of program changes that could be made to the existing system, but some of the most readily apparent ones:

1. **Raise the age of eligibility.** Currently, eligibility begins at sixty-two for early retirement (which has never been changed since early retirement became available in 1956) and sixty-seven for full retirement (moved up from sixty-five with the reforms enacted in the 1980s), and seventy if you choose to wait and receive additional benefits. These could be gradually moved up three years apiece. One of the prime problems today is demographic shift. People

are living longer (now almost eighty years; it was sixty-five when the program started), and the baby boomers are all starting to retire. Birth rates have dropped, so the ratio of workers to retirees is now 2.6 to 1 and dropping down to 2.1 to 1 over the coming years (in the 1950s it was 15 to 1 or more). There are just not enough working people to cover the payments to the retirees. Moving the ages up would be a significant step to solving the problem by changing the ratio of workers to retirees.

2. **Increase the payroll tax rate.** Currently, the Social Security payroll tax (usually listed as FICA on paychecks) is 12.4 percent. Technically, this tax is split evenly between employer and employee, but all economists agree workers bear the full cost of the tax. The payroll tax rate could be raised to help fund future benefit payments. The amount of this increase would be dependent on all the other changes, which, taken together, could fund the shortfall.

3. **Lift the cap on wages.** Currently the maximum income subject to the tax is $160,200. This has been consistently raised over time. This cap could be raised or eliminated, increasing the income into the system, albeit with an increase in marginal tax rates that would cause consider-able harm to the economy..

4. **Means test the benefits.** There are many high-income retirees who get benefits. The benefits are less important to their sustenance compared to those who are lower income and dependent on these payments to live day-to-day. The

Social Security system is already structured so that high-income people are disadvantaged (their payroll tax burdens are much higher, while their benefit payments are only slightly higher), but there could be a further decrease in the benefits as the income levels of beneficiaries rise. There is a good argument that this is unfair for people who have paid in all their lives. However, it could be a reasonable trade-off to achieve a system that is functional and sustainable.

A Better Solution (in the Long Run): Private Accounts

Fixing a bad system might work, but there are better approaches to a permanent solution. One that has been tried successfully in many countries is a private accounts approach. Instead of pay-as-you-go, every person invests in their own private account. This would be managed professionally and would accrue interest and appreciation for the individual owner over time so that when they retire, they have their own nest egg. It would be their property, so when they die, their heirs would get the asset.

There are many advantages. It is safer than the current system, it promotes economic growth, and the benefits would be greater for the individual and would relate to how they fund their own account. There would be minimum payment requirements, with options to add more if investors wanted to give up some current income to invest more for their future retirement. There would also be some controls over the funds, so that they would be present and accounted for upon retirement.

But there is a practical downside to converting to this program. It will require a great deal of capital from some source. If younger workers get to shift their payroll taxes into personal retirement accounts, who will pay taxes to finance benefits for existing retirees and for those who retire before the private accounts are fully funded? This requires a lot of money if the program is launched with no transition period. When the program is complete, it will be a far better system, but how do we get there?

It will take a transition over a number of years to become fully operational. When it is complete, there are no more unfunded obligations, the program will be self-sustaining, and retirees will be in better financial condition.

Outlined here is a conceptual idea of how a transition could work. The specific details would need to be worked out by professionals in the field—but with that caveat, here is the concept.

Social Security Twenty-Year Transition Plan

1. Move 5 percent of an employee's and employer's contributions to their private account in year one, increasing 5 percent each year for twenty years until 100 percent of current payments go into the private account. At that time all contributions will go to an individual's private account, which they will own.
2. Current beneficiaries will continue to receive the same benefits as now from Social Security.

3. As new people retire, they would receive the same payout as currently paid, in part from the Social Security Trust Fund and in part from their private account. When the payout from the private account covers or exceeds the current benefits, then there would be no contribution from the government.

4. There will be a shortfall in Social Security because payments from individuals go partly into their private accounts while current and new retirees continue to be paid part or all from Social Security. This will be covered by three sources:

    a. Increase the employee/employer contributions. This increase all goes into the current trust fund, none to the private accounts. This additional fee endures until the trust fund is no longer needed, then it stops.

    b. Increase the cap on Social Security wages to a certain amount. This stops when the trust fund is no longer needed.

    c. The balance comes from the general revenues of the federal government.

5. Use price indexing instead of wage indexing to determine initial benefit levels.

6. Current and new retirees will continue to receive what they get now. This could be means tested for high-income recipients to reduce the drain on the current system.

7. Optionally, employees can volunteer to have up to 3 percent additionally added to their private accounts, which would be matched by employers.

8. Gradually move the retirement age to seventy and early retirement to sixty-five to minimize the transitional costs. When the plan is fully operational and the current trust fund is no longer needed, the transitional additional charges to cover the shortfall stop (4a and 4b).

9. When an individual is fully on his or her private account, within parameters, the retirement age and benefits can be tailored to their preferences.

10. The private account would be professionally managed by a fiduciary, with several options available to each person. There would be set rules for how the private account could be disbursed.

While this is conceptual, the details and costs could be worked out in a formal proposal by professionals in the field. There may be some costs, dislocations, and unfairness to some extent, but these are necessary evils in moving from a broken plan to one that works.

Bottom Line

The current Social Security program is a financial disaster. The politicians who scream that it cannot be touched are just demagogues pandering to your emotions. The system is broken—badly. It must be touched.

CHAPTER 12

Fixing Medicare

Overview

In this chapter we will focus directly on the problems of Medicare, its future, and how we can address the problems while ensuring that seniors—both today and tomorrow—have a system that provides access to good heath care. Given the broken nature of the current system, it won't be easy, but it must be done.

Like Social Security, Medicare is very costly and must be fixed. The overall program adds over $500 billion in losses to our federal deficit. These losses are growing rapidly and must be controlled if we are to get to fiscal sanity.

Medicare is broken into three main parts:

Medicare Part A is for hospitalization benefits. This is partly funded by the deductions from your pay: 1.45 percent from you with a matching portion from your employer, for a total of 2.9

percent. When you turn sixty-five, you are eligible to enroll in this program, and it will pay 80 percent of your hospital expenses that are controlled by Medicare reimbursement plans. You can elect to purchase private insurance to cover the gap of 20 percent.

Medicare Part B is for doctors and medical expenses. It is optional coverage. The fee you pay is means tested, so the higher your income, the higher the fee to a maximum. As noted in the following, the fees do not come close to covering the costs.

Medicare Part D covers drug expenses. This is also optional coverage. The fees are adjusted as described for Part B.

Brief History

Medicare was enacted in the mid-1960s under President Johnson. Lawmakers were focused on providing medical coverage to the population over sixty-five. Some early supporters did not intend for Medicare to be a debt-subsidized program. It was to be financed by taxes on the individuals and user fees.

But politicians could not resist buying more votes. The program has been expanded many times and has become very dependent on the income taxes paid by all of us, which subsidize the programs by hundreds of billions of dollars every year. That was not the original intention, but that is what has developed over the years. Collectively, Social Security, Medicare, and Medicaid cost about $3 trillion per year and create over $1 trillion per year in federal budget deficits. Medicare alone adds over $500 billion per year to the annual deficit, as taxes and user fees do not cover the costs. As discussed earlier, the benefits planned for the future greatly exceed the income available, which creates the unfunded obligations of the federal government.

Underlying Problems of Medicare

The system is fundamentally broken as it has evolved over the years. In an effort to appeal to voters, Congress has made it into a system that provides care without considering the impact of cost or the negative incentives they built in.

For example, when a beneficiary doesn't pay anything for services, or pays only a small percentage of the costs, there is no motivation not to use the system as much as possible. If you had the opportunity to buy a new car every year, and the government would pay for it no matter the cost, what would you buy? The nicest one around, right? Why not?

Health-care providers are not motivated to keep costs down—just the opposite. The more they do, the more they get reimbursed. And because of possible malpractice lawsuits, they are motivated to get more tests to protect themselves. The tort laws allowing unlimited litigation and damages are a significant problem that drives up costs.

And the older population, especially people at the end of their lives, are the most expensive to care for. There must be some controls over that. Do we really want to spend hundreds of thousands of dollars to prolong a life for a few months? No other countries do that. There are always rules that control the costs of those in the final stages of life.

The incentives are backward, for both patients and doctors, and costs spiral out of control. All of this contributes to a system that is not well thought out and is run by an army of unaccountable bureaucrats who have no incentive to make it more efficient.

Improving the Current System

There have been countless professional studies on the problems of the Medicare system, and innumerable suggestions as to how it can be improved and the future cost/benefit to taxpayers salvaged. The list includes many excellent ideas on reducing costs, few of which ever seem to be enacted, so the program continues and the costs spiral upward and upward. The most recent estimate for unfunded liabilities for Medicare alone is $52.5 trillion over the next seventy-five years. And that estimate grows every year with a new higher estimate.

The details of the many suggestions to fix the current system are so wonky that they are virtually incomprehensible to the average voter, so we will not attempt to explore all of them, but there is one option that deserves some attention.

A Better Way

There is not an agreement as to the best approach, and the political problems of reforming Medicare are immense, but take this as a well-considered alternative to what we are doing today.

The first and most critical provision for any fix: do not throw Grandma over the cliff. We can hear the demagogues already shouting about that. You simply cannot pull the rug out from current needy beneficiaries. To do so is a nonstarter. However, the new program would be available to current beneficiaries as an alternative to the current plan and, if it were to their benefit, they could voluntarily opt into the new program.

In short, converting the entire program over time to a voucher system (technically known as a *premium-support system*) makes a lot of sense. It will not eliminate all the costs of Medicare, but it will control them and change the incentives if properly designed.

A voucher system is one in which beneficiaries receive funding from the government to pay for their own private insurance plan. They would then select their own plan from a number of programs offered by private companies. This may sound radical to some people, but it is basically the same system used now to provide health care to federal bureaucrats and to politicians and their staff in Congress!

Government by its very nature does not do anything efficiently. That is simply a fact. When spending other people's money, the incentives are backward—they will spend whatever they can to appease the public and buy votes. Call us cynical; it is just so.

Bringing private enterprise into the picture and allowing these entities to compete freely across state lines will end up offering the best possible programs for the lowest possible price. And the consumers will pick the best plans for themselves.

Part of the current problem is the cronyism of the present system. The well-funded groups have gotten protections built into the system for their benefit, not for the benefit of us citizens. That must change, no matter what the resolution is to Medicare.

Congress must start doing what is in the best interests of the citizens, not the best interests of the well-funded organizations that can afford expensive lobbyists.

Where Do We Go from Here?

The details of these programs are not simple and need to be carefully thought out and vetted. In the latter chapters, we offer ideas as to how to do that. It is not within the scope of this book to analyze the details of programs; we are here to get the discussion focused and started.

Will we continue to play the fool's game and pretend to fix something that is fundamentally broken, or will we actually fix it?

CHAPTER 13

Fixing Medicaid

Overview

Medicaid is a program originally planned to provide medical care and long-term care for moderate- and low-income individuals whose income is less than 133 percent of the poverty level. It is a joint federal-state program, and the federal government's share (paid to the states) is about 65 percent of the total cost of the program today. State governments administer the program, but under extensive guidelines and control from the federal government.

There is no income source for Medicaid. In other words, Medicaid is not like Social Security or Medicare, which are partly funded by payroll taxes. The federal portion of Medicaid is funded from the general revenues of the government. Spending on Medicaid was $118 billion in 2000. In the fiscal year ending September 30, 2022, the federal portion of this program was $592 billion. It is projected to rise to $879 billion by 2033, per the CBO. It is a major driver of an ever-expanding burden of government, thus contributing to budget deficits, and it is growing rapidly.

The program design does not incentivize states to control costs; just the opposite. Since the federal government finances most of it, states are incentivized to spend more for their constituents.

The program was first enacted in 1965. It has been expanded many times over the years to cover more services and more people with higher incomes. In 2010, the Affordable Care Act (ACA, aka Obamacare) increased spending but did not fix the program's inherent structural flaws. It expanded eligibility, added to the health services covered, and increased the federal share of program costs. It has also spawned other programs such as CHIP (Children's Health Insurance Program).

Total Medicaid enrollment in 1990 was 9 percent of the population; it has grown to over 25 percent today. And as programs were added and expanded, cost estimates have been consistently exceeded by large amounts.

The program covers in-hospital stays, visits to doctor's offices, and prescription drugs, as well a long-term home care.

Major Flaws in the System

The Medicaid system design is very inefficient. There are no incentives for the states or beneficiaries to control costs. The services are provided free of charge with little in the way of copays or deductibles. The recipients also receive free transportation. The generous benefits with few out-of-pocket costs have spurred an overuse of the services.

Originally the program excluded adults with no children unless they were disabled. This was revised by the ACA to include all people under sixty-five years old whose income was below 133 percent of the poverty level, including childless adults.

As a means-tested welfare program, it undercuts work incentives. People are discouraged from increasing their incomes for fear of losing their health coverage. It promotes dependence on government.

Since Medicaid is an open-ended federal matching grant, the states receive additional cash when they expand eligibility or covered services. The states are thus incentivized to expand the program. Because of the heavy match by the federal government, the states have no incentive to reduce waste; they would need to save $2 or more to save the state taxpayers $1. In fact, the incentive is just the opposite—expand to get more federal money. The states have developed many schemes to increase the amount of federal money they receive.

The current federal-state design also undermines political accountability. Neither are fully in charge, so they tend to blame each other for the shortcomings, and the flaws never get fixed by effective reforms.

The formula for funding is based on average per capita income by state. This causes wide variation of funding, with the wealthier states getting disproportionately more. The distribution of Medicaid grants is poorly calibrated to support benefits in lower-income states.

As currently designed, it is also subject to extensive fraud and abuse. Estimates range from 10–20 percent of the funding being fraudulently paid out.[19]

Reforming the System

The program should be reformed for many reasons. Obviously, the fiscal costs are an enormous burden, leading to large increases in the federal deficit. It also causes distortions in the health-care system as a result of the bureaucratically set price structure, which is very complex and expensive to manage. Many providers will not take Medicaid patients because of the program's low fee reimbursements, the complexity in complying with federal administrative practices, and common delays in payment.

The best way to reform Medicaid is to change the entire program to a state-run and state-controlled program, keeping the federal government out of its management and control. The federal government would "block grant" funding to the states on a formula, and the states would design their own programs to satisfy their constituents. This grant would be controlled by the federal government to a set amount. Over time this could be reduced, and the federal fiscal burden could be controlled. Eventually the states could pay for the entire program and be out from under federal control. They would be free to tailor a program that fits the needs of their unique populations.

19 https://www.cnbc.com/2023/03/09/how-medicare-and-medicaid-fraud-became-a-100b-problem-for-the-us.html.

If this plan sounds familiar, it is—it was the approach used by Bill Clinton's very successful welfare reform program in the 1990s. An open-ended entitlement with perverse incentives was replaced by a block grant. The plan was very successful for taxpayers, and it was very good news for poor people. Dependency and poverty both declined, as many welfare recipients were encouraged to become part of the workforce.

CHAPTER 14

Tax Policy

Overview

We should explain why there's discussion of tax in a book that is designed to help people understand the need to control spending. Our main goal is to help people realize that higher taxes are not the right answer—for a wide range of reasons, including the fact that the tax-the-rich approach is mathematically impossible.

As mentioned, the IRS tax code, with all the rulings and interpretations, is 75,000 pages long. *Unintelligible* is perhaps the best description of this colossal tribute to our bureaucracy. But even that may be an understatement.

How did we get to this point, is it good policy, and does it accomplish its goals?

To these observers, the tax code is a testament to ideology, cronyism, and special interests. It is supposed to be progressive, and it actually is for most people. As you can see in the following chart, the top 10 percent of the income spectrum pay most of the taxes, 73.6 percent of the total, and the bottom 50 percent pay little or none, 2.3 percent overall. In fact, many lower-income people don't pay anything—they receive money because the "earned income credit" is actually a form of income redistribution that is laundered through the tax code.

Half of Taxpayers Paid 97.7 Percent of Federal Income Taxes

Shares of Adjusted Gross Income and Federal Income Taxes Paid by Income Group, 2020

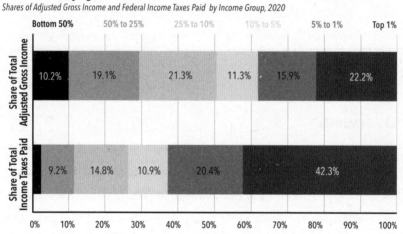

SOURCE: IRS, Statistics of Income, Individual Income Rates and Tax Shares

But the chart only deals with income tax. There are also payroll taxes, namely a 12.4 percent Social Security tax on wages up to $160,200 (this number is adjusted every year based on wage growth) and a 2.9 percent Medicare tax on all wages (these are split between the employer and employee, but effectively the employee pays them all).

The difference between these two major revenue sources is that Social Security and Medicare payroll taxes are dedicated exclusively to finance those old-age programs. Indeed, these are called "social insurance taxes" because politicians want us to think of those payments as being akin to premiums. The fact that there are dedicated taxes is also why some people assert that Social Security and Medicare provide "earned benefits."

Economists usually don't pay much attention to these definitions. Instead, they focus on the degree to which various taxes discourage productive activities such as work, saving, investment, and entrepreneurship (as well as other concerns such as compliance costs and incentives to evade and avoid).

So it makes sense from an economic perspective to look at aggregate tax rates and overall tax burdens. When you look at the total taxes paid by each income quintile (each 20 percent of

The Top 1 Percent Pays About 25 Percent of All Federal Taxes

Shares of Federal Taxes, 1979 to 219

SOURCE: Congressional Budget Office, "The Distribution of Household Income, 2019," Exhibit 16

High-income Households Earn a Disproportionate Share of Pre-tax Income and Pay an Even Higher Share of Total Federal Taxes

SOURCE: Tax Policy Center, *Baseline Share of Federal Taxes*, February 2020
NOTES: Federal taxes include the excise tax, estate tax, corporate income tax, payroll tax, and individual income tax.
Quintiles and pre-tax income are measured by expanded cash income. Each quintile contained one-fifth of the population. Data are for 2019.

©2020 Peter G. Peterson Foundation

income distribution), the numbers are still progressive, but much less so. The highest quintile earns 53 percent of all income and pays 68 percent of all taxes. The lowest quintile earns 4 percent of all income and pays 1 percent of all taxes.

Fair Share

As you can see from these charts, the income and overall tax burden is progressive. It is actually much more progressive than the Nordic countries, which must tax the middle- and lower-income population much more heavily to pay for all of the social and support programs. Just taxing the rich will not produce enough revenue.

We all hear that everyone should pay their "fair share," but what does that mean? We hear the stories about wealthy individuals and corporations that pay no tax, or very low tax rates. Is that "fair"?

Most would say no, and that is a reasonable comment. But how did we get to that point? Those individuals or corporations are just following the tax code. So is the tax code reasonable and fair?

No! It is unreasonable and unfair, and it is a testimony to the abominable mix of special interests and cronyism, all compiled into an unintelligible array of breaks for those with the influence and money to get favorable tax treatment. It is so complex, even the professionals have a hard time finding definitive answers to many questions. President Carter once quipped that the best thing we could do with IRS code is put a match to it and start over. Makes sense to us.

Efficiency vs. Equity

The goal of a tax code and tax policy should be to make taxing a population efficient and equitable. That is very subjective, and there is no perfect way to do that. There will always be some criticisms of any program, no matter how hard they try to make it workable and fair.

Many seem to think the Nordic social systems are good—they offer many welfare benefits and social programs—as is the tax system designed to finance them, at least to some extent. But their tax system is radically different from the US system. For example, their tax rates start imposing maximum tax rates at 1.4 times the average wage, whereas the top tax rate in the US system starts at 8.5 times the average wage. The average income tax rate there is 21.7 percent, whereas in the US it is 11.9 percent. While there are more benefits in Nordic countries, to be comparable the US would have to start the top tax bracket at $85,000 of income instead of $535,000 as it is now. To pay for all the benefits, there is heavy taxation on the middle-, lower-, and upper-income levels. Nordic countries simply cannot generate enough revenue by only taxing the upper incomes. And their "sales tax"—called the Value Added Tax (VAT)—is around 25 percent, vs. around 6 percent here. Their gasoline taxes are very high compared to the US as well.

Is that efficient? Is that fair? There is no simple answer that all would agree on.

Tax Incidence

And what is the "incidence" of the tax? By that we mean, who actually pays the tax (writes the check) and who bears the burden? This is as much a psychological issue as a real one. The best example of this is the corporate tax.

In 2017, the federal corporate tax rate was lowered from one of the highest in the industrial world at 35 percent to a competitive 21 percent. You can hear the politicians and some of the public screaming about corporations not paying their fair share.

Not so fast. First, what is the real incidence of the tax? Who really bears the burden? Every study shows most of the burden is on the employees or the public in the form of lower pay or higher prices. The corporation may write the check, but it isn't impacted very much. It is you and I who pay most of the higher corporate tax. Lowering the tax rate helps attract corporations to grow the economy, instead of shunning them to other countries. The net impact of the reduction in the corporate tax rate was a significant *increase* in corporate tax income. The workers, the consumers, and the government were all better off with the corporate tax reduction.

A Proper Tax Structure

If you ask ten people about the best tax structure, you will get ten different answers. There is no one universal system that everyone would agree on. Let us do our mea culpa now—these are just ideas, and the political arena will make any proposal difficult. There must be compromises to get anything done, if anything can be done for this difficult problem.

Individual Income Tax. The current system is beyond complex—it is incomprehensible. It is so full of loopholes and special interest provisions, trying to patch it makes no sense. Every time there has been a tax simplification program, the tax accountants celebrate—it just keeps getting worse. It's time to start over with some big-picture reform. Fortunately, there are good options.

Flat Tax. A real simplification is in order, and this would do it. A flat tax would eliminate most deductions and loopholes. There would be a simple flat deduction from income to help minimize the impact on lower-income households, and a flat rate on income above that level. The rates would be set to achieve the desired income, but the rates could be lower than now because most of the special deductions would be eliminated. A variation might be to set a few lower rates based on income instead of a flat rate for everyone.

Fair Tax. This is a specific proposal in Congress (HB25) to replace all current taxes with a consumption tax on most goods and services. This has many advantages in that all other taxes are eliminated. With no income or other taxes, record-keeping and tax-preparation cost would virtually disappear, this being a much more efficient way for the government to collect. There would be no payroll taxes, inheritance taxes, corporate taxes . . . all would be replaced.

This is a very pro-growth tax structure. It would be proportional rather than progressive, as all consumption taxes are, so to offset that, a "prebate" has been proposed, which would rebate to all families an amount calculated as the tax on a basic level of consumption each month. A person spending the basic amount would pay the tax, have that offset by the prebate, and effectively pay nothing. The estimated tax rate is 23 percent inclusive (if you pay a retailer $100, $23 of that is the tax). Several independent studies believe that tax rate would have to be higher to replace all the tax income the federal government gets today.

Reform the Current Tax Code. This would become a never-ending struggle to close loopholes and adjust tax rates to become more uniform and "fair." It would entail much political wrangling to have all the special interests protected and might ultimately accomplish little.

Any detailed proposal will be complex beyond the scope of this book. All attempts will be politically difficult to achieve in Congress. As we discuss later, if any progress is to be made, there will need to be a nonpartisan panel of experts who develop the recommendations with a requirement that Congress vote on their proposal. That will not guarantee passage, but it will force

Congress to deal with it. If they don't, the public can speak up at the voting booth.

CHAPTER 15

Federalism

Overview

Our Founding Fathers stood on the shoulders of great thinkers going back to Aristotle. It is clear that they believed in individual freedom and a "classical liberal" economic system, based on personal liberty and limited government.

A good place to start is the Declaration of Independence. Much of the document is concerned with the tyranny of the king and why the Founders believed it necessary and justified to throw off the yoke and become a separate and independent nation. The Founders then met in Philadelphia in the summer of 1787 to lay out a plan for governing this new nation. In 1789, the new Constitution was ratified and a new government was established.

The Constitution was developed as a republican form of government, with the people electing representatives to follow the

Constitution. This unique document was carefully crafted to set up three branches of government with checks and balances to be sure no branch became supreme.

The Constitution also made clear that the federal government was supposed to be limited in size and scope, with just a handful of "enumerated powers." And it specifically states that "the powers not delegated to the United States by the Constitution, nor prohibited by it to the States, are reserved to the States respectively, or to the people."

Federalism

The intentions are clear. The federal government's powers were limited to those in the Constitution and its amendments. The states and the citizens would share all power that was not specifically allocated to the federal government. It would guarantee our rights as well as provide federal policing and a justice system. It would provide for the common defense and many other functions that, out of necessity, need be performed by the federal government.

The Founders almost certainly would not recognize the massive federal government we have today. The many departments and cabinet members, the enormous unaccountable bureaucracy that makes up the rules and regulations, and the massive intrusion of government into our lives, restricting freedom and many of our rights.

The federal/state/individual partnership envisioned by the Founders has been undermined by centralizing so many functions to the federal government that were intended for the states and/ or individuals.

Our liberties as envisioned by the Founders have been curtailed, and the federal government has gone out of control. A sound financial system has been abandoned in favor of massive government spending and deficits financed by massive borrowing.

The Future

It is time to rethink the role of the federal government. We have strayed far from the course outlined by the Founders. The government is slowly evolving into our master, not our servant, as intended by our Founding Fathers. We have gone down an unlighted path. We cannot see the end of the road.

It is time for a major course correction, which will not only move us closer to what the Founders intended but will rein in the cost of government and move us toward fiscal stability. It is not too late, but it is not a moment too soon.

SECTION IV

Common Sense Solutions

Overview

In section I, "The United States Is Bankrupt," we explained the serious problems we face, and must resolve, if we are to survive long-term as a nation. The path we are on leads to insolvency, bankruptcy, and fiscal chaos, whether or not our politicians will admit it.

In section II, "Real-World Fiscal Lessons," we examined multiple countries and policies. It is clear that some policies lead to more growth for a nation and higher living standards for its citizens, while others are clearly harmful to the majority. We took this real-world evidence and extrapolated the best policies for governing a country to improve growth and the lives of its people.

In section III, "What the Hell Can We Do about It?," we explored some conceptual approaches to fixing the most important problems we face, approaches that will lead to a stable and sustainable fiscal climate for this country. The fixes would not only stabilize the country fiscally but would lead to a better climate for growth and thereby boost the well-being of all citizens.

In section IV, "Common Sense Solutions," we explain the economics of what generates growth and prosperity for a country. If we want to fix our crisis in fiscal policy; if we want sustainable growth in our economy for us and our heirs; if we want the future to be secure and sustainable—we need to institute sound policies that will avert our fiscal crisis and insure growth for the future and a rising standard of living for everyone.

CHAPTER 16

Understanding Economic Growth: What Works and What Doesn't

Economic Systems

The starting point is always the nature of the economic system employed. There are two fundamental systems, though in the real world neither operates in a "pure" form.

Free Enterprise/Market Economy

This is frequently referred to as *capitalism*. The major characteristic of this system is individual freedom, with individuals being supreme. The government in this system is constituted by the citizens for their benefit; it is given necessary powers to govern, but does not own the means of production, nor does it control what is produced or the prices that are charged.

This is a "demand-directed" system in that market demand determines what gets produced. The demand is from free individuals—consumers—who express their desires by their willingness to buy goods or services at a given price. This price is a signal to producers; if the price the consumers are willing to pay is adequate for producers to make a profit, then they have an incentive to produce the product. The producers keep the "fruits of their labor."

The ownership of property is private in a market economy. For this to work, there must be laws established to protect individual rights and to protect individuals' property from others. This requires the government to have policing powers and a justice system to enforce the laws. That is what is meant by *rule of law*.

Government's primary roles are to protect the citizens and the borders, to establish laws and regulations, and to enforce the laws through its police powers and a fair justice system. The government needs the ability to raise revenue to pay for these services.

Socialism

Socialism is a different system. In its purest form, there is little individual economic freedom when compared to a market economy. Instead of focusing on the individual, as in a market economy, it is the collective that is supreme. There is little private ownership of property, with government owning the means of production.

Socialism is a "command-directed" economic system in that the government decides what is to be produced at what price, who will get the products, and how much workers will be paid. This is completely under the control of government, as opposed to being controlled by individuals who determine what is produced by what they are willing to buy.

The government is not typically elected by the citizens in fair and impartial elections. If there are elections, they are not open to all parties to run for office, and are essentially sham elections, with the parties in power predetermining the outcomes.

The workers have little incentive to work, as their benefits are not aligned with their effort—they do not reap the rewards for working harder, smarter, or being creative and developing new products.

Mixed Economies

Some forms of socialism might have different labels, such as *democratic socialism*; and some forms of capitalism also might have different labels, such as a *social market economy*. Most nations have economies with some elements of each system.

Some countries are at the extremes of socialist/communist-type systems, such as North Korea or Cuba. Other communist countries are more moderate, employing some elements of a market economy, such as China or Vietnam, even though they are dictatorships in a communist tradition.

Other countries, which are market economies, have substantial social and welfare programs. By all definitions they are free enterprise/market economies. But they include many government programs such as government-run health care or health insurance, heavy old-age benefits, "free" tuition to public educational institutions, childcare benefits, and so on. The list is extensive and varies from country to country, but there are some programs of this nature in almost all market economies, including in the United States.

Government Efficiency

Pardon the oxymoron. There are three points to understand about government:

1. Government is inherently and shockingly inefficient.
2. Insiders and special interests rig government systems.
3. Fraud, waste, and criminality run rampant within governments.

The bigger our government gets, the more these issues multiply. There is no incentive to be efficient when you are spending other people's money. On the contrary, the incentives are to expand government and give away "free stuff" to help one get reelected. Insiders, big business, and special interests have the financial means to gain favor with Congress. Cronyism is rampant in our tax programs, our subsidies, and our laws favoring big business instead of the American people. Between huge programs and an unaccountable bureaucracy, there is much waste and fraud—some of this is well known, but there is no way to measure that which is undetected.

If we are to develop good growth strategies, we must recognize these issues and how we can minimize them.

Fundamental Requirements for Growth

Economies grow when there is an increase in the output of goods and services available to consumers. Output grows when there are incentives to invest in productive resources and the capability (capital) to do so. Virtually all economists would agree on these basic ideas.

In a market economy, it is the private sector that invests in growing output. This is a key function of the private sector—to produce goods and services the public wants and will pay for. The public sector, government, is not in the business of making money and developing more goods and services. When the public sector yields to the temptation to enter into business, a market economy moves toward a socialist economy with government owning the means of production.

It has been tried time and again, all with the same terrible results. Why? Because there is no reward mechanism motivating governments to be creative, productive, and efficient. As noted above, government is inherently and shockingly inefficient—at running business as well as at running itself.

Growing government has many negative repercussions:

1. No matter how well intentioned the programs
   might be, the results of government programs are
   almost never what was intended. There is no
   better example of this than the War on Poverty.

President Johnson intended to help low-income individuals rise to become self-sufficient independent members of society. Sixty years and $25 trillion later, the result is no change in self-sufficiency. Instead, we have a society dependent on government.

2. Governments have nationalized private businesses before. This effort of taking over businesses has always been a colossal failure. In Great Britain, for example, the failure was so complete, Margaret Thatcher privatized most of these with great success. Venezuela took over much of the oil and agricultural industries, which resulted in a complete failure of these industries along with the rest of the country.

3. Enlarging government requires money and resources, and where does the money come from? There are three choices: taxes, borrowing, or printing. All three have dire consequences if growing the economy and raising the standard of living is the goal.

   • If the government balances high expenditures with additional taxes, the budget will be in balance (assuming politicians don't decide to increase spending as well), but it takes capital from the productive sector for the nonproductive sector. This slows economic growth, as there is less capital available to invest in productive resources. Think France.

- If the government does not balance the budget with taxes, it must borrow the money to cover the deficit. This has been the norm for the last sixty years. If the government borrows from the private economy, it is still taking resources from the productive sector for use by the nonproductive sector. In addition, the government incurs debt and the additional cost of interest. If these debts are to be repaid, as they must, significant taxes must eventually be imposed. If the debts continue to pile up (as has been the case in the US), this will eventually lead to bankruptcy. Think Greece.

- If the government does not balance the budget and elects to print money to pay for the deficits instead of borrowing from private sources, the money supply is expanded. If growth in the money supply is faster than growth in economic output, the result is inflation. The bigger the deficit and the more money we print, the higher the inflation. Think Argentina.

Government that is constituted to benefit the welfare of its citizens has certain requirements that it must meet. Beyond that, there are other desirable functions that it could perform. It could operate some welfare programs for those who are not able to care for themselves. It could operate pension and retirement programs for the benefit of the elderly. The list of services it *could* do is extensive; the question then becomes what it *should* do.

What we have observed can serve as guidance to what works best. It is clear that limited, smaller government leaves more capital in private hands to invest and grow output. It is clear that government should limit its functioning to the basics of its responsibilities and let companies have the freedom to operate within a normal range of constraints. It is clear that government is less wasteful when there is Federalism. It is also clear that excessive regulation strangles the productivity of business. And finally, it is clear that when a government lives within its means, it avoids the debts that must be eventually paid by future taxes on future generations.

The Formula for Growth

The formula for growth is quite simple. Just follow these steps:

1. Save
2. Invest
3. Produce
4. Consume

To maximize growth, you minimize the "government take" and maximize public saving and investing. That is how to effectively grow an economy. This is the formula that works best:

SMALLER GOVERNMENT + LOWER TAXES +
BALANCED BUDGET =
MORE INVESTMENT & FASTER GROWTH

CHAPTER 17

What Can I Do about It?

ongress is used to handling its legislative role as the entity
that proposes and executes spending programs for the
United States. In the early years of this country, we were blessed
with wise statesmen who were focused on the best interests of the
country. They were prudent in their expenditures and were not
in favor of big debts. Here are a few comments from some of our
Founders and other politicians on this subject:

*"As a very important source of strength and security, cherish public credit.
One method of preserving it is, to use it as sparingly as possible; avoiding
occasions of expense by cultivating peace, but remembering also that
timely disbursements to prepare for danger frequently prevent much
greater disbursements to repel it; avoiding likewise the accumulation of
debt, not only by shunning occasions of expense, but by vigorous exertions*

in time of peace to discharge the debts, which unavoidable wars may have occasioned, not ungenerously throwing upon posterity the burden, which we ourselves ought to bear."

—GEORGE WASHINGTON

"I am for a government rigorously frugal & simple, applying all the possible savings of the public revenue to the discharge of the national debt; and not for a multiplication of officers & salaries merely to make partisans, & for increasing, by every device, the public debt, on the principle of it's being a public blessing."

—THOMAS JEFFERSON

"I wish it were possible to obtain a single amendment to our constitution. I would be willing to depend on that alone for the reduction of the administration of our government to the genuine principles of its constitution; I mean an additional article, taking from the federal government the power of borrowing."

—THOMAS JEFFERSON

"The principle of spending money to be paid by posterity, under the name of funding, is but swindling futurity on a large scale."

—THOMAS JEFFERSON

"And to preserve their independence, we must not let our rulers load us with perpetual debt. We must make our election between economy and liberty, or profusion and servitude. If we run into such debts, as that we must be taxed in our meat and in our drink, in our necessaries and our comforts, in our labors and our amusements, for our callings and our creeds, as the people of England are, our people, like them, must come to labor sixteen hours in the twenty-four, give the earnings of fifteen of these to the government for their debts and daily expenses; and the sixteenth being insufficient to afford us bread, we must live, as they now do, on oatmeal and potatoes; have no time to think, no means of calling the mismanagers to account; but be glad to obtain subsistence by hiring ourselves to rivet their chains on the necks of our fellow-sufferers."

—THOMAS JEFFERSON

"The consequences arising from the continual accumulation of public debts in other countries ought to admonish us to be careful to prevent their growth in our own."

—JOHN ADAMS

"For several years past the revenues of the government have been unequal to its expenditures, and consequently loan after loan, sometimes direct and sometimes indirect in form, has been resorted to. By this means a new national debt has been created, and is still growing on us with a rapidity fearful to contemplate—a rapidity only reasonably to be expected in a time of war. This state of things has been produced by a prevailing unwillingness

either to increase the tariff or resort to direct taxation. But the one or the other must come. Coming expenditures must be met, and the present debt must be paid; and money cannot always be borrowed for these objects. The system of loans is but temporary in its nature, and must soon explode. It is a system not only ruinous while it lasts, but one that must soon fail and leave us destitute. As an individual who undertakes to live by borrowing soon finds his original means devoured by interest, and, next, no one left to borrow from, so must it be with a government. We repeat, then, that a tariff sufficient for revenue, or a direct tax, must soon be resorted to; and, indeed, we believe this alternative is now denied by no one."

—ABRAHAM LINCOLN

"I want the people of America to be able to work less for the government and more for themselves."

—CALVIN COOLIDGE

"Solvency is maintained by means of a national debt, on the principle, 'If you will not lend me the money, how can I pay you?'"

—RALPH WALDO EMERSON

"We don't have a trillion-dollar debt because we haven't taxed enough; we have a trillion-dollar debt because we spend too much."

—RONALD REAGAN

Unfortunately, we are not blessed with such statesmen-politicians today. Only a few of our elected representatives are focused on what's best for the country; most are focused on what is best for themselves. And that is to get elected and reelected. It is natural to do what is in one's best interest, but when it comes to the future, it is time to put country ahead of personal goals. If representatives cannot do that then they should stay home and let someone who will take their place.

The result of the politics of today is debt quagmire resulting from "well-intentioned" programs that are popular among the electorate. They sprinkle benefits generously to the many, without regard to the real-world effects, and in the process the burden of government expands and enormous debts are accumulated, with no means to pay them other than to borrow more money—the great Ponzi scheme.

Hope Is Not a Plan

The real world of politics today makes it clear that self-discipline is not going to impose itself on our leadership. No one is brushing fairy dust over Congress to magically fix this problem. But there are ways to get our fiscal house in order.

It starts with us. First, we have to understand the problem and where we, as a country, are headed. We have tried to help with that in earlier parts of this book. Then we need to look at the real world and see the impact of good and bad economic policy. We have tried to do that in earlier parts of this book as well.

With this information, we need to shout to our members of Congress to fix the fiscal insanity before the ship of state collides with the iceberg and we all sink together. The question remains: Once we manage to get our politicians' attention, what should they do to clean up the mess? Here are a few suggestions.

Balanced Budget Amendment

There have been many attempts to pass a balanced budget amendment to the Constitution. None has worked. An effort is underway at the time of writing this book. Perhaps it will succeed, but so far it has not. As reasonable as the idea sounds, it has its flaws: namely, it is focused on the wrong thing in this era of excessive spending. And there are always provisions for exceptions and emergencies. That opens the door to keep on piling up debt. It would be better than nothing, but not the best solution.

Consider that forty-nine of fifty states have some sort of balanced budget requirement. Does that stop big government and wasteful spending in states such as New York, Illinois, Massachusetts, and California? Sadly, no. If anything, such requirements simply give politicians an excuse to raise taxes.

Our real problem is too much spending as a result of an aging population, poorly designed entitlement programs, a self-seeking desire by politicians to promise all our citizens "two chickens in every pot," and a Congress with no discipline. It is a Congress, to paraphrase Alexis de Tocqueville, that is bribing citizens with its own money to buy votes.

Plus, if we balance the budget with exorbitant taxation, it will destroy the growth of the country to the long-term detriment of all of us. Fiscal restraint and sound economic programs are needed for the long-term good of the nation. The balanced budget amendments, where instituted, have not been effective long-term.

Debt Brake/Spending Cap

This is a program that sets a maximum increase in government spending each year, say 1 or 2 percent per year. This is a simple, flexible rule that allows Congress to add more in one area if they compensate elsewhere. If we control the growth of government to modest levels, and the economy grows faster, the debt slowly becomes less significant as it relates to the total economy. The debt to GDP ratio will slowly decline. Switzerland has implemented this kind of plan for many years with great success, as has Colorado.

Fixing Broken Programs

Seventy percent of federal spending is on autopilot, the so-called nondiscretionary spending. Most of these entitlement programs are broken and dysfunctional today. Because of our aging demographics, programs that did work in the past are no longer economically viable. We have explained this in detail.

We all should recognize by now that we have an enormous problem that must be fixed. Our goal is to be sure the citizens of this country understand this reality and what can be done to fix it. Then we must demand of our representatives that it be fixed, or we will elect someone who will.

CHAPTER 18

Public Support + Political Action = Solution

Alexis de Tocqueville was a French lawyer and politician who toured our new country in the early 1800s. In 1835 he wrote a glowing account of the fledgling nation, *Democracy in America*. One phrase widely ascribed to de Tocqueville (and which is turning out to be prophetic) is this: "The American republic will endure until politicians discover that they can bribe the public with their own money."

Sadly, that is happening today. Our elected representatives are too focused on getting elected and reelected. So they "bribe" the public with all sorts of goodies and programs to gain favor and buy votes. They, and we, have lost all sense of what makes for good government—or even what the purpose of government is. This has led us to a fiscal cul-de-sac with out-of-control spending and never-ending deficits.

Politicians may have good intentions, but the results rarely yield the intended results. Simply stated, governments are inherently inefficient. But there are degrees of incompetence. The federal government is the worst, as it is most removed from the people. As such, we have an enormous unaccountable bureaucracy that has taken control of much of our lives. It is too easy for them to squander our tax money.

This system isn't working; we need to see that clearly. When we do, then and only then will we be able to crawl out of the economic morass that we have today.

Public Support Is the Answer

Abraham Lincoln once wisely observed: "With public support we can get anything done." The American public must understand the problems we are facing and support changes to fix them.

The problems are immense and complex, we all understand that. Throughout this book we have tried to identify the most important of them, but there are many others. We have given real-world examples of policies that work well and those that have proven disastrous. We can learn much from this history.

We have also suggested some conceptual ideas to help fix the problems. We are not pretending there is only one solution, but we do think there is only one successful approach: we need to slow the growth of the federal government.

The Case for a Commission

One potential strategy is to have Congress and the executive branch coordinate to create a spending-control commission of experts in the various areas that need to be addressed. This should be done through an act of Congress, signed by the president. This commission would be required to submit its findings and recommendations in the form of actual legislation that Congress and the president would act on. That does not necessarily mean that they must accept every recommendation as submitted—or accept any at all—but they must review and modify as they see appropriate, then vote. They should not be allowed the option to duck the responsibility of voting and being counted, regardless of what their decision is.

That will only happen if we, the people, demand it. We must support the formation of a commission to address our fiscal problems, difficult though they may be.

It is not too late, but it is not a moment too soon. The Bowles-Simpson Commission was appointed by President Obama for this purpose. It didn't work because there was no public support for the changes and no teeth to force Congress to deal with the recommendations. Most of the major recommendations were never enacted or even considered by Congress. Since that approach relied heavily on higher taxes, we should be thankful.

But that does not mean the concept of a blue-ribbon commission (with a requirement that Congress give its recommendations an up or down vote) is wrong. We need answers and accountability, and we need them right now.

Conclusion

The debt bomb's fuse is lit, and it is burning rapidly. We know the bomb will blow eventually, and the great Ponzi scheme will end. That happens when the world realizes that the United States cannot service its debts. Then the investors of the world will lose confidence in us and stop buying in. If we allow that to happen, it will be the end of this country as we know it. There are no good solutions once we reach that point.

Make no mistake—that is the path we are on. Even the Department of the Treasury says so in its published financial statements: "The current fiscal path is unsustainable."

We have let this go far too long. There are no easy answers, but we must have the fortitude to recognize the problem and deal with it. We must dig deep for difficult solutions before it is too late. Complacency is our enemy.

If we continue to convince ourselves that there is no serious problem, that we always find a solution and we will again when the need arises; or that there is nothing we, as individual citizens, can do ("I am just one vote—what difference can I make?"); or that we can kick the can down the road for our heirs to deal with . . . If we allow ourselves to be seduced by these tempting delusions, we will reach a point when there is no longer a workable solution available—it will be too late. We will be helpless, and economic catastrophe will rain down upon us. This country will no longer be the one we inherited, and future generations will pay the price of our economic malfeasance and complacency.

It is not too late. Economic disaster can be avoided. But it is up to us, the voting public, to understand the issues and make sure our elected representatives develop sound economic policies that will get us back on track to a sound economy and a prosperous future. If they will not fix the problem, we must vote for someone who will.

Listen, learn, understand, act. That is our job.

That is why we must support both the commission and the difficult spending decisions that must be made. If we don't do that, if we don't support those difficult changes to entitlement spending and government borrowing, if Congress continues down the unsustainable path, we will hit the proverbial iceberg and sink. The debt bomb will have exploded.

Don't let that happen on our watch.